George John Whyte-Melville

The Queen's Maries

A Romance of Holyrood

George John Whyte-Melville

The Queen's Maries
A Romance of Holyrood

ISBN/EAN: 9783744777339

Printed in Europe, USA, Canada, Australia, Japan

Cover: Foto ©ninafisch / pixelio.de

More available books at **www.hansebooks.com**

THE QUEEN'S MARIES.

A ROMANCE OF HOLYROOD.

BY

G. J. WHYTE MELVILLE,

AUTHOR OF 'DIGBY GRAND,' 'THE INTERPRETER,' 'HOLMBY HOUSE,'
'GOOD FOR NOTHING,' ETC.

VOLUME II.

LONDON:
PARKER, SON, AND BOURN, WEST STRAND.
1862.

LONDON:
PRINTED BY G. PHIPPS, 13 & 14, TOTHILL STREET,
WESTMINSTER.

THE QUEEN'S MARIES.
A ROMANCE OF HOLYROOD.

'Yestreen the Queen had four Maries,
 The day she'll hae but three,
There was Mary Beton, and Mary Seton,
 And Mary Carmichael, and me.'

CHAPTER XXII.

'"And grant me his life!" Lady Margaret cried;
 "Oh! grant but his life to me!
And I'll give ye my gold and my lands so wide,
 An' ye let my love go free.

'"And spare me his life!" Lady Margaret prest,
 "As ye hope for a pardon above;
And I'll give ye the heart from out of my breast
 For the life of my own true love!"'

ALTHOUGH the gayest of the gay where revelry was in the ascendant, and gifted with that tameless courage and those qualities of endurance, which were the characteristics of her family, alas! too often proved in the reverses of that ill-fated line, Mary Stuart was subject to constitutional fits of dejection, the more painful that she struggled bravely against the incubus; and, however much it may have darkened her spirits, never suffered it to affect her temper. The Queen was always kind, considerate, and smiling towards her household, even while her eyes were full of tears, and her heart was sore with undefined anxieties and anticipations of evil for which she saw no obvious cause. Her Majesty was generally more free from such depressing influences at St. Andrew's than elsewhere. The keen sea-breezes of that bracing locality seemed to have a favourable effect upon her health, and she enjoyed, above all things, the absence of state and ceremony, on which she specially insisted in the old cathedral town. Fond as she was of the saddle, it was a great pleasure to the beautiful Queen to gallop over the spacious sands that skirt St. Andrew's Bay, where she could enjoy a stretch of two miles and more, to the mouth of the river Eden, careering along on the firm hard surface, with the spray of the German Ocean wet on her cheek, and her horse's feet splashing amongst the spent waves of the receding tide. Then she delighted to fly her hawk at the wild fowl abounding a mile or so inland, returning by the well-known chain of grassy, sandy hillocks, that are there called links, and devoted in modern times by the Scottish gentry to their national recreation of golf. Sometimes crossing the Eden at the shallows near its mouth, she would roam over the waste of low grounds that stretch to the northward, perhaps as far as a small straggling hamlet, in days of old a Roman settlement, defended by one of their masterly encampments, and called by the legions, *Lochores*, a Latinism which the

Scottish peasant of to-day reproduces in the name of Leuchars.

Then, on her return from these joyous expeditions to the small house in the South-street, selected for her own royal residence, she gathered her few intimates and friends around her, and passed the evenings in amusement and hilarity, from which the very name of business was rigidly excluded.

To one who was so staunch a supporter of the Faith in which she had been brought up, not the least attractive feature in this picturesque town was its beautiful Cathedral, that goodly edifice, which the over-zealous followers of John Knox thought it no sacrilege to devastate, and of which a fine ruin alone remains to suggest to us what it must once have been.

The antiquary prowling about the moss-grown flag-stones that pave its aisles, or prying into nooks and corners of sinking buttress and mouldering wall, finds memory sharpened and curiosity stimulated at every turn. The philosopher, contemplating the length and breadth of that spacious area, heretofore rich with the decorations of architecture, and glowing in the pomp and pageantry of Romish piety, recalls the solemn music, the swinging censers, the carven images, the twinkling lights, the florid altar, the gilded crozier, and the mitred abbot, with his train of monks and choristers winding solemnly up the dusky nave. He speculates, half pitying, half sneering, on the various modes in which men offer their homage to the true God,—the Mollah exhorting the faithful Moslem from a minaret, the priest pattering Latin in a corner before a crucifix, the precentor's nasal psalmody quavering within the unsightly walls of a Presbyterian meeting-house,—and he reflects that the forms of religion change like the fashion of a garment, and that the offertory of yesterday becomes the superstition of to-day and the mummery of to-morrow; but the Christian, looking upward to that ruined arch, through the stained glass of which, as through a prism, the light was wont to stream with rainbow colouring, sees the blue sky of heaven smiling changeless in its span, and rejoices to believe that clear as the blessed light of day is the light of piety, penetrating the disguises and the ceremonials and the ignorant prejudices of weak humanity, like the sunshine that vivifies as surely the dusky slab lurking in the gloomiest corner of the Cathedral, as the fresh daisy raising its head on the free mountain-side. What matters the fashion of the cup, chased in gold, or of broken pottery, so the parched lips can but drain their fill of the waters of life?

It was the Queen's habit to devote the early part of the day to such affairs of state as would not excuse neglect, even at St. Andrew's, and to the usual household duties, which every lady in the land, royalty included, then found to occupy a considerable portion of her time. At twelve, she dined temperately and hastily, after which she mounted her horse, and, accompanied by as small a retinue as possible, devoted the afternoon to exercise and amusement.

It was on the second day after her arrival at St. Andrew's that she agreed to Mary Hamilton's request, who begged that she might be allowed to accompany her Mistress in the daily ride. The Queen had seen with concern the sad change that had come over her favourite's looks, and although surprised at this departure from her usual habits (for the maid-of-honour was a timid and unskilful horse-woman), willingly acceded to a proposal that promised to bring back the colour to her cheek and the light to her eye. With a couple of men-at-arms and a page, as their sole escort, they left the town by its southern gate, taking the horse-track that led to the broad expanse of Magus-Muir, a locality destined in subsequent troubles to obtain an odious celebrity for the murder of Archbishop Sharpe at the hands of the Covenanters, but only interesting to Mary and her courtiers that it was rich in an abundance of wild fowl.

Chastelâr had been already tried on the charge of high treason and sentenced to death; he was to be beheaded the following morning at day-break. It was perhaps natural that neither Mary nor her maid-of-honour should have exchanged a syllable concerning his fate.

The Queen was riding 'Black Agnes.' As soon as they were clear of the town, she put her horse into a gallop, and never drew bridle for several miles. It did not, however, escape Her Majesty's observation that the animal on which Mary Hamilton was mounted, a bay of great strength and spirit, usually uncontrollable by the gentle hand of a lady, was going in a perfectly docile and collected form; also, that the girl seemed to-day perfectly free from the timidity which commonly left her miles behind her Mistress in these scampers across a country. They had already lost sight of the sea, and had gained a wild inland district of moss and moor, varied here and there with patches of cultivation, and interspersed with a few fir-trees of stunted growth, and an occasional cairn of stones breaking the level skyline, when the Queen pulled up at the top of an acclivity, and pointing to a solitary horseman stationed, as if expecting them, at the foot of the slope, observed to her companion, with a wild attempt at cheerfulness obviously forced—

'You scarcely thought, Mary, I was entrapping you to witness a *rendezvous*. It is a romantic spot for the purpose, nevertheless, and yonder is the gallant who has kept tryst with me as he promised, faithfully enough.'

Mary Hamilton would have felt it an unspeakable relief to have burst into tears. The whole fabric of her morning's work was swept away by the sight of that plain dark figure so stationary yonder, on his horse. She would have given her life for half-an-hour's conversation with the Queen alone, although (strange inconsistency) she dared not ask her indulgent Mistress point-blank to accord her that trifling favour, and now, this hateful stranger would probably hang about them all day, and to-morrow it would be too late! A thousand shadowy and incongruous impossibilities crossed her brain, too, at the same moment, all turning upon the one sickening certainty, that even while she grasped at their consolations, she felt too surely it would be out of mortal power to avert. She answered with a ghastly smile that startled the Queen, and totally unconscious of what she said the while,

'Let us go to meet him, Madam; it may be that he can give us some hope.'

Mary stared at her attendant vaguely, and shook her

head, then, putting her horse in motion, descended the slope towards the solitary traveller, flushing a brace of wary old moor-fowl and a curlew, while she plunged and scrambled with characteristic fearlessness through the broken ground that intervened.

The horseman dismounted as she approached, and did her homage with a grave dignified air, not without something of caustic humour that recognized the peculiarity of the situation.

'I might not fail to do your Grace's bidding,' said he, ' even in so light a matter, as to see you fly your hawk on Magus-Muir, but in good faith, Madam, a younger cavalier could scarce have ridden harder than I have done since sunrise, and my old bones ache to some purpose for my punctuality.'

'Nay, master Knox,' answered the Queen, with marked favour, ' those of your blood have been ever willing to set foot in stirrup at the bidding of the Stuart, and I have been taught to believe that a black cassock may cover as stout a heart and as loyal, as a steel breast-plate. Behold, I have here a fitting reward for your punctuality, to be given with the cordial good-wishes of your Queen.'

Thus speaking, Mary drew from her bosom a crystal watch of curious and elaborate workmanship, large, substantial, and of considerable thickness, but esteemed a triumph of mechanical ingenuity, and presented it to the gratified Churchman, with a charm of manner that increased the value of the gift a thousand-fold.

He bowed low over the royal hand that proffered so flattering a favour, and mounted his horse once more with an air of extreme satisfaction and the ready alacrity of a youth.

So far all was progressing smoothly, but Mary Stuart, judging of the human temperament by her own, was persuaded that the exhilarating influence of a gallop would produce the mollifying results she desired, and render even stern John Knox malleable to the purpose she had in view.

'Ye are not so strict,' said Mary, 'but that ye like well to see a fair flight, and I have a hawk here, master Knox, that hath not her equal on the wing this side the sea; nay,' she added playfully, as he seemed about to excuse himself, and muttered something of 'business' and 'distance,' 'ye have thought fit to reprove all my other amusements, my feastings and fiddlings and masquings and such-like, nor have I borne you any grudge, for that I believed you to be sincere, but ye love a good horse well I know, and can reclaim a hawk, for all your solemn bearing and grave studies, with the best of us. By these gloves, I will never forgive ye, an' ye join not my pastime to-day.'

Thus speaking, the Queen signed to her page, who came up with a beautiful falcon on his wrist. The bird was transferred to Her Majesty, and seemed to shake its bells more gaily, and raise its hooded head more proudly, as though it knew and loved the hand that sleeked its neck-plumage with so gentle a caress.

The Churchman was nothing loth. Despite a weak frame and failing health, his bold ardent nature, the same disposition that under different circumstances would have made him a soldier, a statesman, an explorer, or an adventurer, bade him take delight in the free air of the moor-land and the stride of a good horse. He settled himself in the saddle, gathered his reins, and professed his readiness to attend Her Majesty.

'These creatures,' said he, arguing down some scruples of his own, which much enhanced the promised gratification, 'are given for our lawful recreation. Man is doubtless lord over the beasts of the field. I will stay to witness one flight of that long-winged falcon, 'tis a goodly bird indeed if I know aught of the craft. One flight, and so crave your Majesty's license to depart.'

The Queen smiled her assent, and galloped merrily on to a waste marshy surface, where the tramp of their horses ere long flushed a wisp of wild-fowl, and Mary, throwing her hawk in the air, was soon scouring over the moor at a break-neck pace, her eyes fixed on the sky and her whole attention absorbed by the gyrations of her favourite.

John Knox, too, casting aside for the moment his cares and responsibilities, entered into the sport with the eagerness of a boy. It was seldom indeed that zealous man shared in any of the lighter amusements of the time, but in pleasure as in business, whatever he found to do master Knox went about with his whole heart and soul. The wrinkles seemed to smoothe themselves on his brow as the wild wind swept back his thin grey locks, and he felt ten years younger, while the blood leapt warm in every pulse, and he urged his steed forward with leg and rein in the excitement of the flight.

Mary Hamilton rode like a woman in a dream. The bay horse, accustomed to fret and chafe under the re-

straining influence of the bit, seemed bewildered by his
unusual freedom. He had plunged and bounded away
with his head in the air, according to his wont, prepared for a contest in which he was sure to obtain the
mastery, and he may or may not have been disappointed
to find that his rider's carelessness of consequences ex-
ceeded his own, and that he was suffered to exhaust his
mettle far more rapidly than he expected. With a
stony white face, and her abundant hair streaming over
her shoulders, the maid-of-honour sat back in the
saddle and flew along at a pace that even 'Black Agnes'
could not surpass, unconscious apparently of amusement,
or danger, or excitement, or any thing but the relief
afforded to her mental anguish by the physical sense of
being carried with such velocity through the air. When
the mallard was struck to earth at last, and the horses
were pulled up, with panting sides and dilated nostrils,
and wild eyes all a-glow with excitement, the Queen
gazed on her reckless attendant in surprise, and even
the severe Reformer remonstrated with her, Popish
damsel though she were, for the utter disregard in which
she seemed to hold that white neck of hers, and the
probability of breaking it in such a headlong career.

'Fair mistress,' quoth master Knox, ' there is reason
in all things ; over caution supposes want of faith, but
the contrary extreme, such as you have exhibited to-
day, denotes presumption and fool-hardiness. You are
young; humanly speaking you have many years before
you. You would not willingly be cut off like a flower
in its bloom. Why should you thus risk your life as if
there was no to-morrow ? '

She did not seem to hear him. She answered nothing, but the last word of his sentence seeme 1 to strike some chord within her, for she turned away muttering below her breath, ' To-morrow. It will be too late tomorrow,' and clasped her hands upon her breast as if in pain. John Knox did not observe her, for his attention was now taken up by the Queen, who seeing in his face, which was bright with repressed excitement, that the propitious moment had arrived, motioned him to her side, and moving her palfrey out of ear-shot of the others, broached the subject that had led her to invite him thus to join in her favourite amusement.

' I have brought ye a long ride, master Knox,' she said, ' and I would ye could return and taste a cup of sack at our poor lodging in St. Andrew's, but I know your busy avocations, and that ye will not willingly be absent from Edinburgh a day longer than is necessary. Ere you depart, I would fain ask your opinion on a subject of toleration.'

At the ominous word, the Divine's whole countenance changed as the sky changes after a chance blink of sunshine in December. The clouds of controversy gathered on his brow, and suspicion gleamed in his cold piercing eyes. The Queen saw the storm brewing, and added, with a pleading sweetness few men would have been able to resist, ' The sun smiles on all alike, the blessed rain of heaven falls on the just and on the unjust. Which of us shall penetrate our neighbour's motives, or judge our neighbour's heart ? '

' Ye shall have no dealings with the ungodly,' replied Knox, hastily, with an instinctive prescience of what was coming; ' the Amalekite is to be smitten root and branch till he be destroyed out of the land.

But I anticipate your Grace, and have not yet been favoured with your commands.'

He took himself up shortly, as though aware and a little ashamed of his ill-manners. The Queen, reining in her horse, proceeded with great earnestness,

'The spring is now approaching, and you know with what devotion we, of the Catholic faith, look forward to the solemnities of Easter. I am not ashamed to solicit your interest that my fellow-religionists should be suffered to observe that festival, with their accustomed ceremonies, unmolested. I know too well the feelings of the party who call themselves the Reformed Church. I know (none better, and ye cannot deny that I have reason) master Knox's influence with that powerful majority, and his Sovereign entreats him thus in confidence to exert it in the cause of charity and peace and good-will amongst men.'

It was a powerful appeal from a monarch to a subject, especially under the peculiar circumstances of the moment. Riding alone over the breezy upland with that beautiful woman, under the exciting influences of wild scenery and an inspiriting gallop, the heart softened by the smile of nature, and the blood tingling with exercise, few men but would have found it impossible to resist a suppliant, who was at the same time a Queen, and *such* a Queen. Loyalty demanded obedience, self-interest whispered the advantages of royal favour, and the impolicy of refusing a Sovereign, ambition drew a dazzling picture of the eventual triumph of the cause wrought out by the judicious concessions of one man alone, and that man venerated as the Great Pillar of Protestantism in Europe; but conscience thundered

'No;' and to do Knox justice, he never wavered nor hesitated for an instant. His lineaments looked more rugged, his brow more uncompromising than usual, when he rejoined,

'Your Grace has addressed me frankly, and as frankly I reply to you,—If by holding up my finger I could retain for the Church of Rome any one of the privileges that are daily and hourly slipping from her grasp, if by so doing I could relieve her from one of the least of the indignities or calamities which are surely gathering round her head from the four quarters of heaven, see, Madam, as I ride here a living man before you, I would keep it clenched down by force till the nail grew through the palm of my hand! I am a soldier, I will not desert my banner; I am an heir, I will not alienate my birthright; I am an honest man, I will do my duty at all hazards, in the face of every prince in Europe.'

He looked sublime while he spoke; the weak, ungainly figure reared itself in the saddle with all the pride of a Colossus, and never a belted earl could have borne a nobler front in coronet and ermine than did that Minister of the Church in the fearless integrity of his purpose. Mary grew pale with anger and disappointment, nevertheless she had long since learned the painful lesson of self-control, and she forced herself to speak calmly, while her very blood was boiling within.

'Would ye refuse to others the liberty of worship ye exact for yourselves? Would ye persecute men, who differ from you only in their mode of worship, more ruthlessly than the Pagan Emperors persecuted those early Christians who were our teachers as well as yours? Bethink ye, master Knox, this is a world of change. The old faith hath many staunch supporters still. Men's minds may alter as they have altered ere now, and those who are all-powerful to-day may find themselves petitioners for mercy to-morrow. Is it well to exasperate beyond endurance those who may in their turn come to have the upper hand?'

The implied threat was injudicious and ill-timed; she would have done better, knowing with whom she had to deal, either to have given vent to her indignation and defied him outright, or to have repressed it altogether; but she was only a woman after all, and womanlike, could not entirely separate the two sensations of anger and fear, so she adopted those half-measures to which her sex is fain to have recourse in a difficulty, and roused his spirit while she tried to work upon his apprehensions.

'I defy the Romish Antichrist as I defy the principle of evil itself,' replied Knox, with kindling eyes and excited gestures. 'Am I watchman set upon a hill, and shall I leave my post because the enemy is at hand? Am I shepherd in the wilderness, and shall I abandon my flock because the storm is gathering on the horizon? No, Madam, once again I tell you that if you count on my allegiance in this matter, I renounce it; if you depend on my loyalty, I am a rebel!'

'It seems so,' she replied very coldly, and yet there was a tone of utter sadness and desolation in her voice that smote on the Churchman's heart. With looks of tender pity and concern, such as a father bends upon a favourite child, he would have argued with her once more, would fain have expounded to her the fallacies of her doctrines, and recalled her from the way which he conscientiously believed to be the very high-road to destruction; but as is often the case in such disputes, the more one yielded the more the other encroached, and she cut him short with haughty impatience, reining in her horse, and pointing with outstretched arm towards the south.

'Yonder lies your homeward way, master Knox,' said the Queen, 'and here is mine; I sent for you to listen to my proposals not to hear your pulpit declamations at second-hand. When next we meet others may have found means to tame that haughty spirit, and the avowed rebel may be glad to solicit pardon from his Sovereign. I have no further need of you, you may depart!'

The dismissal was as peremptory as it was unceremonious; though burning to reply and charged with argument, he could not pretend to misunderstand it, and unwillingly withdrew. Ere the tramp of his horse had died out on the heathery sward, Mary burst into a passion of tears which she could no longer control; then bending her head low to her horse's neck, put 'Black Agnes' once more to her speed, and followed by her attendants, galloped off in the direction of St. Andrew's.

Independent of her own private sorrows and distresses, the Queen's political position was at this time one of peculiar difficulty and anxiety. A sincere Catholic, and consequently from the very nature of her faith an ardent upholder of its infallibility and advocate for proselytism, she was compelled by the exigencies of her station to give countenance to its most determined

foes. Not only did she see its tenets repudiated by
the great majority of her people, but the very toleration they extorted for themselves was denied to her,
and it was a subject of open discontent that the Mass
which had been suppressed elsewhere was suffered to be
performed in the Queen's own chapel at Holyrood. The
very adviser on whom she placed the utmost reliance,
her half-brother the Earl of Moray, was the chief support of the Protestant party in her kingdom. And
although Seton and a few more of her nobility remained
secretly attached to the old faith, their number was
comparatively trifling, and their zeal scarcely proof
against the temptations of ambition and self-interest.

Then, as if her difficulties were not sufficiently per-
plexing without foreign interference, her relatives, the
Guises, lost no opportunity of reminding her that they
looked to her alone for the restoration of the Religion
in Scotland, and eventually over the whole of Britain;
whilst a strong party in Spain furnishing her, for aid,
with nothing but unasked advice, actually reproached her
for lukewarmness in the cause to which she was sacri-
ficing day by day her authority, her comfort, her very
safety, and to which she was so sincerely attached
that rather than resign it she would have lost, as she
afterwards did lose, her crown, aye, and the head that
it encircled.

The insults levelled at her person through her
belief, constantly goaded her to anger which pruden-
tial considerations urged her to suppress, and when
pictures were paraded before her in the streets, ridi-
culing all that she held most sacred, and priests mal-
treated in her own chapel for the performance of their

ritual and hers, it is painful to imagine the feelings of a sensitive woman and a Queen compelled to forego her revenge, and even to court the favour of those undutiful subjects who had originated such overt and outrageous scandal.

No wonder she galloped on with burning cheeks and swelling heart, reflecting only on the failure of her benevolent scheme so thwarted by the obstinate integrity of Knox, and insensible as the very horse that carried her, to the beautiful scene opened out at her very feet.

Before her lay the noble sweep of St. Andrew's Bay, framed as it were in its golden sands, that stretched far to the north along the coast of Forfarshire till their tawny line was lost in the distant ocean at the jutting promontory of the Red-head. Clear against the blue expanse, dotted here and there with a white sail, rose the delicate pinnacles of the Cathedral, supported on the right by the bluff square tower of St. Regulus, firm and massive like some bold champion, proud yet careful of his charge. On the left, far out into the water, stood the sea-girt defences of the Castle, while between these prominent objects many a graceful arch and pointed spire denoted the churches and colleges adorning that stronghold of learning and piety, refining the taste with their exalted beauty, whilst they carried the eye upward towards heaven. Below these, the smiling town, with its white houses and gardens, scattered more and more as they neared the water, straggled downwards to the beach; and beyond all, the broad sea lay, calm and mighty in the serenity of its majestic repose.

On her bridle-hand, Mary might have scanned the wide champaign of two counties, through which two rivers ran in parallel lines to the ocean, the intermediate space dotted with woods and rich in cultivation, the river Eden gleaming like silver in the foreground, the smoke of Dundee floating white against the dark heights of Forfarshire, as it followed the downward current of the Tay, and in the far distance, the dim outline of the noble Grampians, losing their misty tops amongst the clouds that streaked the placid sky.

Yet Mary marked nothing of this. With a flushed cheek, with a drooping head, and, oh! with a cruel sorrow at her heart, she galloped on, and never checked her pace nor addressed her attendants till she reached the gate of the ecclesiastical city once more.

Then she drew rein, and as they rode together up the South-street, she blamed herself that she had not sooner observed and taken pity on Mary Hamilton's obvious exhaustion both of mind and body.

The bay horse was, ere this, reduced to a state of abject submission and docility; the bridle, on which he was wont to strain so eagerly, lay loose upon his neck, and he seemed to be looking about for his stable with a very wistful expression of fatigue and discomfiture; but his rider's face was pale and rigid, while her eye was wide open and her mouth firmly set; she seemed unconscious of all that was passing around her, and disclosed that vacant, yet pitiful expression of face which is only to be seen in those who walk in their sleep, or who are undergoing some racking torture of mind by which their outer faculties are benumbed.

'You are weary, child,' said the Queen, kindly. 'I should have remembered you are not so indefatigable a rider as myself. Well, we are at home now, and I shall not require you again this evening.'

So speaking, the Queen leapt lightly from her palfrey, and flung the rein to the attending page, but as she did so she looked once more in the face of Mary Hamilton, who was dismounting, and something she saw there made her start back, and exclaim, in an agitated whisper,

'What is it? child! You frighten me! What is it?'

The other found her voice at last, but it came husky and broken to her lips.

'For mercy sake, Madam!' said she, 'let me unrobe you; my kind Mistress, do not deny me this one favour! let me unrobe you, and alone.'

The Queen though still startled, blushed vividly as something crossed her mind, that yet seemed partly to re-assure her, and she beckoned her maid-of-honour to follow as she entered her private apartments, then dismissing her other attendants, threw herself into a chair, and with the colour not yet faded from her brow, bade Mary Hamilton unburthen herself of this dreadful grief that was weighing on her mind.

A burst of hysterical weeping was the result, but it calmed and relieved the sufferer until she could find words in which to offer her petition and tell her pitiful tale. Women are wonderfully patient of such affections in their own sex, and the harshest of them will be gentle and considerate with one of these outbreaks that they have agreed to call 'nervous attacks.' Much more so, kindly Mary Stuart; soothing her attendant like a child, she soon restored her to sufficient composure to make intelligible the boon she had all day been striving to entreat. What this was an hour or two would disclose; in the mean time, the Queen and her maiden sat whispering in the darkening twilight, till the shafts and pinnacles of the neighbouring Cathedral loomed grim and fantastic in the shadows of nightfall, and the light in the sacristan's window told that the time of Vespers was already past.

At the same hour John Knox riding steadily along the road to Edinburgh was beguiling the gloomy journey with a proud recollection of his resistance to the Queen's advances, sternly reminding his conscience that animosity to the Papists was a Christian's duty, and that forgiveness was no Christian virtue to one of another faith.

And Chastelâr in his dungeon was preparing for death by reflection on the pitiless beauty of her in whose face he would never look again.

CHAPTER XXIII.

'While hate itself is fain to shrink,
Love freely ventures—lose or win—
And friendship shivers on the brink,
Where love leaps boldly in.'

THE wind was rising out at sea with fitful sullen moans; the town of St. Andrew's was wrapped in thick darkness, save that at long intervals a light glimmered from some lofty window showing where the pale student bent over his weary labour; the gathering waves rolled in with increasing volume, breaking heavily against the rocky base of the old Castle; but the sentinel at its eastern angle though he felt the spray wet on his face, could not distinguish the white surf leaping and boiling down yonder in the dark gulf at his feet; the vaulted chambers, the winding stairs and gloomy corridors of that stronghold were cold and dismal enough; but what of the dungeons down below the water-line, where the light of day had never penetrated yet, where the salt froth oozed and trickled from the bare rock, and the clammy slime stood on its chill surface like the death-drops on the brow of a corpse? Aye, what of the dungeons? Ask those who were forced down the narrow stair with pinioned arms and muffled faces, knowing that their feet would never ascend the slippery steps again! Ask those who were immured in narrow cells, hollowed like living sepulchres from the rock, and so built in that the soul indeed might, but the body never could, escape from its imprisonment! Ask those who were let down by a cord into the black, loathsome pit from which they never came out alive! The answer may perhaps some day be spoken in tones of thunder before earth and heaven.

Even now they tell you how the marks of blood remain in evidence on that accursed keep; how the very stones bear witness to a foul and murderous deed, none the less guilty that victim and perpetrators were equally steeped to the lips in homicide and crime; that it was the accomplishment of Divine vengeance and the fulfilment of a Martyr's prophecy.

When the proud Cardinal, leaning over his window to behold the frightful holocaust at his ease, smiled bitterly on George Wishart at the stake, did not his heart sink within him to hear the Martyr's solemn denunciation?.

'David Beatoun, though the flames shall lick up my blood, yet shall thine remain to stain the very wall on which thou leanest, as a witness against thee till the Day of Judgment!'

When the Laird of Grange and the two Leslies dragged their enemy from his bed and slew him at that very window, must not remorse have whispered in the moment of despair that there is a retribution even here on earth? and when we learn that the fierce murderers did actually hang his body over the wall, as a butcher hangs a carcase in the shambles, till the blood soaked and sank into the very stone-work, and that centuries have not washed out its stains, what can we say but that the Divine Will doth not always postpone justice to a future world, and that Divine vengeance seldom fails to work out its own precept, 'Whoso sheddeth man's blood by man shall his blood be shed.'

The only cheerful apartment in the Castle was the guard-room; although the night was dark and stormy, the wind sighing and the waves beating without, a huge wood-fire blazed and crackled in the ample chimney, reddening the weatherbeaten faces of the men-at-arms, and glancing fitfully from their shining head-pieces and bright steel corslets. Small care had these rude hearts for the weather without or the woe within; the spray might dash against their casement, and the weary prisoner moan his wrongs in the neighbouring cell.

'What would you have? 'tis but the fortune of war,' quoth the soldier; 'my luck to-day, yours to-morrow; a bed of heather for this one, a lair of straw for that; a free discharge and a fresh enlistment at last. Put another log on the fire; I wish we had got something more to drink.'

Their Captain sat somewhat apart, his head resting on his hand, and his sheathed broad-sword lying idle on the floor. As the flame flickered on his forehead a frown seemed to pass and repass across its surface, but his eyes were intently fixed on the red glow of the embers, and perhaps he was drawing pictures that had no semblance of reality in their glare.

A moody man of late was Alexander Ogilvy; once the best of comrades and the blithest of merry-makers; he was becoming captious, contradictory and quarrelsome. The hand stole to the sword-hilt now on the lightest word of provocation, and although he was still ready to pledge his brethren-in-arms with the wine-cup, it seemed to be no longer the desire of good-fellowship that stimulated him, but a fierce, morose thirst that he was resolved to slake in gloomy defiance.

Perhaps some of the phantoms he was watching in the fire might have accounted for this untoward change in the young soldier; perhaps it was not pleasant to picture to himself in those glowing depths the stately figure of Mary Beton, with her flowing skirts and quivering ruff, bending her lofty head so graciously towards a sharp spare man in gorgeous apparel, with a clever face and a sneer, that if Ogilvy had ever formed any idea of Mephistopheles, would have presented to his mind's eye the very expression of that sarcastic personage; perhaps it did not enhance the harmony of the group to recognise in the hottest corner, a figure bearing a grotesque resemblance to himself, watching the pair with jealous supervision, and presenting the undignified, if not ridiculous exterior, of one who runs second in the race of love.

With a movement of impatience he drove his heavy heel against the logs, dispelling the whole representation at a blow, and causing the fire to burn out fiercely and the sparks to fly in thousands up the chimney.

At this moment a man-at-arms entered the guard-room, and approaching his captain informed him that two persons at the gate demanded admittance.

'Impossible,' said Ogilvy; the wicket is locked and the watch set; bid them go to the devil.'

'One of them bears the Queen's signet,' answered the man, 'though she winna let it out of her hand. I doubt it's one of the leddies,' he added, ' an' I ken the t'ither yane fine ; it's daft James Geddes, the fule.'

This altered matters considerably. The royal signet ring was esteemed a voucher for any one who bore it, and all guards, warders, and such officers of the Sovereign, had strict orders to consider it in the light of a direct communication from Majesty itself. So Ogilvy, taking down a torch from the wall, proceeded to the wicket in person.

On arriving there he encountered a female figure, cloaked and hooded, that after a moment's hesitation he recognized as Mary Hamilton, and half-watching over her, half sheltering himself behind her, much after the manner of a faithful dog, but with less expression of countenance than that sagacious animal, the ungainly figure and broad unmeaning face of James Geddes, the fool.

Ogilvy knew the maid-of-honour personally well enough ; also, on the universal principle, (for though she was not the rose to him, she had been *near* the rose,) he was disposed to oblige her for the sake of Mary Beton, and bowing courteously, begged to know if she had any authority, at that late hour, to enter the Castle.

'I have come to visit a prisoner,' replied she in a hard set voice, showing him at the same time the Queen's signet-ring, which James Geddes watched as if he expected the Captain of the Guard would swallow it at a gulp.

Ogilvy bowed and withdrew the many bolts and bars

that secured the wicket, then calling a soldier to fasten
them again, preceded his visitors along the vaulted passage that led from the entrance to the guard-room. Mary
Hamilton shuddered as she heard the gate clang to behind her; and the fool looked more than half inclined to
draw back and abandon his adventure at the outset, but
a glance at his protectress reassured the latter, and the
former, seeming as it were by a violent effort to adopt
a fresh part, assumed an air of gaiety and carelessness
strangely at variance with her bloodless face and horror-stricken eyes.

Arrived in the light of the guard-room she produced
an ample stone bottle from beneath her cloak, and
placed it on the rude oak table.

'The Queen has not sent me to visit her brave soldiers
empty-handed,' said she, with a wild dreary smile.
'While I am about Her Majesty's business I hope they
will drink Her Majesty's health.'

The fool's eyes glistened at the sight of the liquor,
but once more he glanced at Mary Hamilton, as the
well-trained dog looks at its owner ere he ventures to
touch the tempting morsel placed before him. The
soldiers gathered round with well-pleased faces; the
bonds of discipline were not at that period drawn so
tightly as at present, and a carouse was a sufficiently
acceptable variety to the monotony of a night on guard.
Ogilvy, too, who might, under other circumstances,
have objected to such an employment of those he commanded, for the reason we have before hinted at, was
unwilling to disoblige one of the maids-of-honour, and
set the example himself by filling a cup to the brim
with the strong fiery liquor, and emptying it to the

Queen's health. James Geddes prepared to make sport for the rude soldiery, and one and all disposed themselves around the table for an hour or two of conviviality.

The fool, although habitually not averse to imbibing as much drink as he could honestly come by, seemed, on the present occasion, unusually cautious in his potations, and whilst he encouraged the laughing soldiers to drink deep from the stone jar, only put his own lips to the cup that was freely offered him, and for once appeared resolved to keep his poor faculties as keenly as possible on the alert. He glanced, too, ever and anon, at the door by which Mary Hamilton had left the guard-room, and seemed to watch and listen attentively for the slightest noise.

It was painful to see the gleams of anxiety that broke at intervals through the dense stupidity of his broad flat face. At such times his countenance again assumed the wistful sagacity of a dumb animal, and instinct seemed to warn him that he must summon all his faculties to meet some vague catastrophe for which his reason was unable to prepare.

The soldiers jested with the poor half-witted creature according to their wont, and as their draughts began to ascend into the brain proceeded to coarse practical jokes and much boisterous mirth, of which his infirmities were made the butt. James Geddes, however, never relaxed from his vigilance. Sometimes a lurid gleam shone for an instant in his eyes as a grossly offensive insult penetrated even his obtuse nature, and occasionally he gave vent to his feelings by a low moaning noise and the rocking of his body to and fro, as was his custom when more than commonly irritated or distressed, but he was always careful to fill the soldiers' cups for them to the brim, was always watchful of the demeanour and presence of their commander; and whilst his glance wandered furtively to the door, his whole attention seemed painfully on the stretch to catch the sounds of that voice which it was his nature to obey with the attachment and fidelity of a dog.

Mary Hamilton, after exchanging a few words in a low tone with the Captain of the Guard, in which an acute observer might have detected successively the accents of remonstrance, entreaty, and command, had produced a small lamp from beneath her cloak, and lit it at Ogilvy's torch; then taking a key from his hand, which he seemed to deliver very unwillingly, proceeded alone towards the dungeon, casting over her shoulder one glance at the fool, in which caution was speakingly impressed, as she departed. The soldiers were already launched on their carouse, and Ogilvy, though he seemed watchful and restless, often starting from his seat and taking short turns up and down the guard-room, joined at intervals in their revelry.

The maid-of-honour stepped cautiously down the winding-stair that led to the dungeon. Mary Hamilton had nerved herself for the undertaking on which she had embarked, and now that she was fairly within the dreaded Castle of St. Andrew's, the agitation which had rendered her so helpless all day, had given place to the calm, resolute bearing of one who is prepared to succeed in a hazardous enterprise, or die in the attempt. It was indeed a trying situation for a young tender-hearted woman. The man she loved lay in that loathsome dungeon, condemned to die; she believed that she alone could save him. She had the means and the opportunity; all must depend on her courage and presence of mind. Yes, she would save him, and her reward would be to see him prostrate himself at the feet of another! It was a bitter thought, and yet she never wavered for an instant.

As she reached the door of his cell she thought she heard his voice, the well-known voice, rich and melodious even here, and the sound of her own name made her pause and listen. He was consoling himself in his prison, this man who was to die on the morrow, with the illusions of his art. He had composed a ballad, of which her name was the refrain, and was singing it to himself in his cell.

'There's a bonny wild rose on the mountain side,
      Mary Hamilton,
In the glare of noon she hath drooped and died,
      Mary Hamilton;
Soft and still is the evening shower,
Pattering kindly on brake and bower;
But it falls too late for the perished flower,
      Mary Hamilton.

'There's a lamb lies lost at the head of the glen,
      Mary Hamilton,
Lost and missed from shieling and pen,
      Mary Hamilton;
The shepherd has sought it in toil and heat,
And sore he strove when he heard it bleat,
Ere he wins to the lamb it lies dead at his feet,
      Mary Hamilton.

'The mist is gathering ghostly and chill,
            Mary Hamilton,
And the weary maid cometh down from the hill,
            Mary Hamilton,
The weary maid but she's home at last,
And she trieth the door, but the door is fast,
For the sun is down and the curfew past,
            Mary Hamilton.

'Too late for the rose the evening rain,
            Mary Hamilton,
Too late for the lamb, the shepherd's pain,
            Mary Hamilton,
Too late at the door the maiden's stroke,
Too late for the plea when the doom hath been spoke,
Too late the balm when the heart is broke,
            Mary Hamilton.'

She heard it every word, and for a time her composure gave way. A burst of passionate weeping relieved her, and drying her eyes she unlocked the door and entered the dungeon.

The light she carried streamed on Chastelâr's figure, dressed in the very clothes in which she had seen him taken. He was half sitting, half lying, in the extreme corner where the stone was dryest, and took no notice of her entrance, thinking it was the gaoler, but continued to hum the air he had just been singing. When he lifted his eyes, however, and recognised his visitor, he rose at once, with his habitual courtesy, and bade her welcome to his habitation, laughing pleasantly the while.

'You find me poorly lodged, mistress Hamilton,' said the poet, 'and although I live in a castle I am but scantly provided with room. It is not for long, however, as to-morrow morning, I am informed, they mean to remove me to a narrower chamber still.'

She could not bear to see him thus; again the warm tears filled her eyes as she gasped,

'The doom has gone forth, I heard of it to-day; there is but one chance left.'

He smiled a sweet, sad smile.

'I have done with chances now,' said he; 'I set my all on one cast and I do not complain that the luck has gone against me. It was kind of you to come and visit me, Mary,' he dwelt fondly on the name and repeated it more than once, 'I was thinking of you even when you appeared. I was wishing I could see you once more. What of the Queen?' he added, with an eager glance. 'Is she here at St. Andrew's?'

'She sent me to you this very night,' replied the other. 'What I do is by her command, and, according to her directions. You shall not die, Chastelâr; she bade me save you, and we have the means, only be obedient and, above all, keep silent.'

His whole face lighted up as he seized her hand and covered it with kisses. Life was sweet to the poet, with his warm impulsive nature and his glowing hopes; all the more so when he learned that he would owe that life to the favour of the Queen. He listened eagerly while the maid-of-honour detailed to him the proposed manner of his escape, which indeed seemed feasible enough. She hoped, through the potency of the brandy which she had left behind her in the guard-room and with the assistance of her half-witted confederate, to bring the soldiers to a state of hilarity at which the eye is not very keen nor the suspicions very easily aroused; while in her whispered conversation with Ogilvy she had already, with the unscrupulous shrewdness of a woman, made use of his attachment to Mary Beton to win him half over to her enterprise. She calculated on his at least ignoring her proceedings; she then proposed to dress Chastelâr in her own hood and mantle which, as their statures were not very dissimilar, would form a thorough disguise, and she had sedulously tutored James Geddes, who took an unaccountable delight in the whole proceeding, to conduct the captive to the gate with the same deference and care as if it were herself. It was difficult to make the faithful fool understand this part of the plan, but she had instilled it into him at last. He was to encourage the inebriety of the men-at-arms to the utmost of his power, and directly Ogilvy's back was turned to go his rounds, which something she had told him would induce the Captain to do at an earlier hour than usual, James Geddes was to return to the dungeon and summon the visitor to depart. Chastelâr, in Mary Hamilton's clothes, would then accompany him to the gate and she herself would remain a prisoner in his place.

'And when they find you here,' exclaimed the poet, all his generous impulses protesting against such an arrangement, 'think of Ogilvy's rage! think of the rude drunken soldiers! It cannot, it shall not be! Your life would have to pay the penalty.'

'And I would give my life freely for yours,' she replied, a bright smile breaking over her face, causing her to look for the first time to-night like the Mary Hamilton he remembered in the Queen's chamber, when all was so different and so happy.

'For mine!' he repeated, with a sadly troubled face.
'Oh! too late! too late!'

'Do not say so,' she continued, speaking very rapidly and eagerly, with her slender fingers grasping the prisoner's arm like a vice; 'I would not have told you this but that we shall never meet again. The very terms on which the Queen yielded to my entreaties were these —that you leave Scotland within twenty-four hours, and pledge your honour never to enter Mary Stuart's dominions more. Oh! if you knew how I knelt and prayed and pleaded ere I could wring from her the token that gave me access here; if you could have seen her angry frown while I implored, or heard the cold resolute voice in which she said at last, "I consent, but only on these terms, that I never behold him more," you would have pitied me, Chastelâr; you should pity me now, for though I have saved your life, oh! I am very, very miserable.'

Again she burst into a fit of weeping, the hot tears fell upon his hand, but he heeded them not, he scarce seemed conscious of the devoted broken-hearted woman trembling there before him; the Queen's words struck like a poniard to his heart, and he was mad! love-mad once more!

He broke rudely from his companion, he flung her hand from his arm, as if the touch were a viper's, his eye glared, and he ground his teeth together in the agony of a wounded spirit, and a pride humbled to the dust.

'I scorn her mercy!' he shouted, in wild frantic tones, 'I renounce her pardon, and I refuse her terms! Tell Mary Stuart, from me, from Chastelâr, who will be led out to die at sun-rise to-morrow, that the last words he said were these—"If every one of these hairs were a life," he passed his fingers while he spoke through the abundance of his dark clustering locks, "I would lose them all, ere I would accept the smallest, lightest token of the Queen's favour. Because I have dared to love her more dearly than man ever loved woman here on earth, because I love her wildly, fondly, madly, still." Ha! ha! she cannot rob me of that! Queen though she be, she cannot recall the past! Mary! Mary! ere to-morrow's sun be set, that cold heart shall ache, as it hath never ached yet, and Chastelâr will have had his revenge!'

And now the pure unselfish nature of Mary Hamilton's character rose superior to the crisis. Another who had loved him less would have turned away in wrathful scorn and left him to his fate: not so, that gentle faithful heart; on her knees she besought him to listen to reason, to yield himself to her guidance, to accept of life for her sake.

The moments were very precious. Already James Geddes was beating impatiently at the door, warning them that he had fulfilled his ministering in the guard-room, and that Ogilvy was absent for the nonce. She clung to him—she urged him—she implored him, and the man was obdurate, pitiless of himself as of her, hardened in his despair, reckless, miserable, and resolved to die.

How many before and since have been like him? How many have turned obstinately from the pleasant easy path of safety and contentment, to reach wildly at the impossible, scaling the slippery crag just so high as shall dash them to pieces in their fall? There are spirits that seem ever destined to be striving after the unattainable, doomed in a punishment more cruel than that of Tantalus to thirst for a *mirage*, that is never even within the bounds of hope. Be it love, wealth, ambition, their craving seems to be in its very nature insatiable, and perhaps even were the wildest and most extravagant of their desires to be granted, they would but turn aside indifferently as if success must needs be loathsome, and long incontinently for something else that could never be their own.

It is well for the philosopher who has learned to create for himself his life's essentials. Blessed is the Barmecide who can make believe that the tasteless water from his earthen pitcher, is a draught of nectar from a cup of gold. But woe to the sanguine enthusiast who cannot be convinced that 'half a loaf is better than no bread,' the fool who shouts 'all or none' for his war-cry, while he runs a tilt against the invincible windmill of conventionalism, and getting, as he deserves, none instead of all, has every bone in his body broken into the bargain for his pains.

Mary Hamilton pleaded for dear life; far dearer, indeed, was that life to her than her own. James Geddes hearing her sobs and broken accents, became so importunate at the door of the cell, that one or two drunken soldiers from the guard-room, aroused by the noise, came loitering down the dungeon-stair, and at the same moment Ogilvy, not in the best of humours, returned from his rounds, and the last chance was gone for evermore.

Whether the Captain had met with any disappointment in visiting the different posts under his charge, or whether he had reason to suppose that his midnight walk was to be more agreeable than usual, and felt aggrieved to find its dulness unrelieved by any variety; it is not our province to enquire; but he certainly showed more zeal for discipline than on his departure, and entering Chastelâr's cell in person, after kicking poor Geddes away with a bitter curse, ordered the maid-of-honour imperatively to be gone, and summoned two of the soberest men-at-arms to mount sentry for the rest of the night at the head of the stair.

Mary Hamilton neither screamed, nor fainted, nor wept. She knew that all was over now, and accepted the inevitable catastrophe with that resignation which Providence seems to bestow in mercy on those who are destined to endure great suffering. She bent over Chastelâr's hand as she bade him a silent farewell, and though her lips moved as if in prayer not a sound escaped them. Then she raised her head proudly and walked rigidly and slowly out of the cell, less like a living being than a figure set in motion by mechanical means. The boisterous men-at-arms in the guard-room stood aside respectfully to let her pass, and James Geddes as he followed her cowered and shook with a mysterious fear.

But Chastelâr, in the selfishness of his great love, so strong even at the threshold of the grave, scarcely noticed her; nay, he even called out to her as she departed with a message for the Queen. The ruling passion was indeed strong in death. As his short and brilliant life had been valued only for her sake, so she was his last thought now that he stood on the brink of eternity.

'Tell her,' he said, ' that I commend me to her with my last breath. Thank her for all her kindness, and the mercy she would have shown me even to-night, but say that I choose to die rather than be banished from her presence, and so Chastelâr bids her farewell,—the fairest, the proudest, and the best beloved Princess under Heaven!'

He seemed composed, even cheerful. To all appearance, the man was in possession of his faculties and in his right mind, yet these were the last words Chastelâr ever spoke on earth.

CHAPTER XXIV.

'They led him forth to the silent square,
  In the gray of the morning sky,
And they brought him a cup of the red wine there,
  To drink, and then to die.

'Without the gate Lady Margaret stood,
  And she watched for the rising sun,
Till it blushed on the stone-work, and gleamed on the wood,
  And the headsman's work was done.

'Not a limb she stirred; but when noon-day's glow,
  Smote fierce on her temples bare,
A brighter sun had not melted the snow
  That streaked Lady Margaret's hair.'

———

HE morning broke dull and gloomy; the wind that had been blowing steadily all night had subsided towards dawn, but a chill easterly breeze was still creeping in from sea-ward, and a light vapour rested on the surface of the ocean, beneath which the lead-coloured waves rose and sank in the sullen monotony of a ground swell. Little by little the cheerless dawn stole imperceptibly over the rugged bluffs and scaurs that to the northward formed a bulwark for the town, and disclosed at every minute new rents and fissures in

their sea-worn sides,—new wisps of dripping sea-weed trailing in ungainly streaks across their slippery surface; the ebbing tide, too, receding as though unwillingly, with many a landward leap and backward whirl, disclosed here and there round black rocks, peering like the heads of sea-monsters above the restless waters, while a solitary sea-mew, turning on its white wing downward from the cliff, screamed as it were in disappointment of its fishing after the storm.

The Castle walls rose sullenly against the misty sky; black, massive, and impenetrable, they suggested no feelings but those of inhospitable and uncompromising grandeur. Their battlements, weather-stained with the gales of centuries, frowned dark defiance down on the ruffled ocean, and the royal flag with the golden lion of Scotland ramping in its folds, half-unfurled and dripping with last night's brine, flapped drearily and heavily in the fitful breeze.

To and fro for a space of some twenty yards under the wall, a female figure was pacing with swift irregular steps, and her fingers twining convulsively as she held her hands clasped together before her. Mantle and dress were wet and disordered from the inclemency of the past night, but the hood of the former covered her to the brows, and it was only by the lower part of her white, rigid face that a passer-by, had there been one at that early hour, could have recognised Mary Hamilton.

In a sheltered corner, screened from the wind by a massive buttress, cowered the ungainly figure of James Geddes; rocking himself backwards and forwards, he moaned as if in pain, and blew upon his cold fingers, huddling himself together for warmth the while, but his eyes travelled wistfully after Mary Hamilton as she walked, and though she seemed unconscious of his presence, they never quitted her figure for a moment.

Once when close to him she paused in a listening attitude, and he took courage to address her, whining like a troubled child,—

'Will ye no gang hame? will ye no gang hame? 'Tis cauld an' dreary biding here for sunrise. I'm wantin' hame; I'm wantin' hame!'

She startled violently when he spoke, but turning from him in impatience, only walked backwards and forwards faster than before.

And now a dull knocking might be heard in the square of the Castle, and the noise as of heavy beams put in motion, broke the stillness of the early morning. At each fresh sound Mary Hamilton stopped in her walk and started on again as if goaded to exertion by internal agony; the fool shivering and moaning in his corner yet still watching her intently, at length rocked himself off into a fitful half-slumber, waking up at intervals to implore his unheeding companion to go home.

Within the Castle preparations were already making for some grave and unusual event. The soldiers, though flushed and fevered after their debauch, yet preserved an ominous silence, and betrayed on their coarse faces an expression of pity and dismay. Ogilvy himself looked pale and sorrowful. Once when he caught sight of a sharp polished instrument propped carefully that its edge should not be frayed against a corner, a tear might have been seen to steal down the Captain's cheek till it hung in his heavy moustache; but his voice was gruffer than usual as he gave some necessary order a minute afterwards, ashamed doubtless, as men commonly are, of those emotions which betray that they have a heart.

Two or three workmen had been already admitted at the wicket, and were taking advantage of the increasing light to erect an ominous fabric of boards and scaffolding in the centre of the Castle square. They went about their job in a prompt business-like manner enough, but they spoke in whispers, and when a basket of saw-dust was brought out, it was disposed almost reverently in its place. After this a taint of Death seemed to pervade the atmosphere, and one of the artificers, a strapping young fellow six feet high, had recourse to a dram of strong waters on the spot.

Down below in his dungeon Chastelâr was asleep. Strange as it may appear men always *do* sleep before execution. Be it that the faculties are so completely worn out by the wear and tear of anxiety that usually precedes condemnation, or be it another instance of the Divine mercy which would fain shorten that time of agony to the sufferer, such is the fact; and in the last moments of criminals it is almost invariably the case that body and soul both taste their last repose on earth, ere the one sleeps and the other wakes for all eternity.

What were the poet's dreams in that short welcome rest? Did he anticipate the great change, and fancy his spirit already free from its prison, wandering through those unknown regions which good Eneas and rich Tullus and Ancus, and your grandfather and mine, and a host of those we both knew and valued and would have followed into any danger or on any expedition, have ere this thoroughly explored—to which you and I, though we think so little about it, are bound just as surely and inevitably, and with which to-morrow, or the day after, or this time next year, we may be familiarly acquainted? Or did he retrograde to the past, and revel and ruffle it at Holyrood once more, riding the sorrel horse alongside of 'Black Agnes,' and sunning himself in the bright eyes of the Maries, and above all the smiles of her their peerless Queen? Perhaps a vision of that face he had worshipped so fondly shone on him for the last time kindlier and lovelier than it had ever appeared in reality, and to wake from such a dream as that was so bitter that even death became welcome as promising sleep again.

The knocking on the scaffolding failed to arouse him, and when Ogilvy went gently into his cell with a torch, the soldier passed the light half pitifully, half admiringly over the manly face that could look so calm and peaceful at such a time.

And in the royal house in the South-street, within a culverin's distance of the Castle, were all the inmates sleeping soundly at the dawn of that gloomy morning? Was that a bed of rest, on each post of which was carved a crown, and at the head of which the arms of Scotland were emblazoned so richly in embroidery and cloth of gold? Was the lovely face so flushed and troubled thus buried in the pillows to exclude the light of day; were the white hands pressed against the throbbing temples and covering the beautiful little ears, in dread of the morning gun which would be fired at sun-rise and tell that all was over?

It was no fault of Mary Stuart's that Chastelâr was doomed. All that lay in her power had been done to save him; all that royal dignity and womanly shame would permit. Perhaps she believed him to have escaped even at the last; she would hardly guess at such infatuation as he had shown even in *him*, and yet the victim's sleep had probably been far sounder than hers for whom he was about to die.

Lights were burning in the Queen's chamber, heavy curtains at the window excluded the faintest glimpse of dawn, yet she was turning and tossing restlessly on her couch, while Chastelâr was pacing in grave composure up the dungeon-stair that led into the grey morning, the last he would see on earth.

But one bed at least in the royal house remained cold and unoccupied—Mary Hamilton had never returned home all night. Under the Castle wall she kept her weary watch, and as the dawn widened into day, she was still pacing hurriedly up and down, up and down, and at every fresh turn casting a horror-stricken look towards the sky.

Presently the mist rolled slowly away, curling downwards from the heights of Craigton and the bleak outline of Drum-Carro hill, disclosing the bare and cheerless table-land that forms the eastern boundary of Fife. The changing wind cleared the loaded atmosphere, and glimpses of blue became apparent through the fleecy vapours dispersing rapidly as they were driven out to sea; already the beams of morning were gilding the sands of the bay, and two or three fishing-boats hoisting their white sails were putting out hopefully from the shore; the cheery voices of the sailors came pleasantly over the water, and reached the ears of the watcher under the Castle wall. Still the hood was drawn over her face; still she paced with that monotonous tread up and down, up and down; still the poor fool crouching under his buttress, moaned and rocked and shivered, urging pitifully that he was 'wantin' hame—wantin' hame.'

Then, though the Castle yet remained a huge black mass in deep shadow, spire and pinnacle on the Cathedral began to blush and glow in the morning sun; presently when Mary Hamilton turned in her walk, her eye was dazzled by his horizontal beams streaming along a pathway of molten gold as he rose cloudless from the sea. Retracing her steps she saw the whole massive building before her shine out at once in a flood of warm yellow light; then she stopped short, bending forward with her hand outstretched, and listening eagerly.

Comforted by the warmth the fool rose from his lair, and rubbed his hands together with an attempt at cheerfulness, shifting alternately from one foot to the other in a kind of measured dance, and striving in his vacant half-witted manner to attract the attention of his companion.

She neither moved nor noticed him; still in the same attitude, with her neck bent forward, her hand stretched out, and the lower part of her face visible beneath her hood, white and rigid as if cut from marble.

He pulled her cloak impatiently,—'Come awa' hame,' he whimpered like a child left alone in the dark. 'I'm feared here—I'm feared here; it's no sae canny sin' the dawn.

> 'Wi' a rising wind,
> And a tide coming in,
> There's a death to be;
> When the wind's gaed back,
> An' the tide's at the slack,
> There's a spirit free.'

He crooned this doggrel over twice or thrice, pointing at the same time to the wet sand below them and the black shining rocks left bare by the ebb; but she never answered him, for ere he was silent the heavy boom of a culverin broke on the morning stillness, and a wreath of white smoke rising above the walls of the Castle floated calmly and peacefully out to sea. The fool cowered down and hid his face in his hands. She did not start—she did not shriek, nor faint, nor quiver, but she threw her hood back and looked wildly upward, gasping for air; then as the rising sun shone on her bare head, Mary Hamilton's raven hair was all streaked and patched with grey.

CHAPTER XXV.

'" How should I your true love know
From another one?"
" By his cockle hat and staff
And his sandal-shoon."'

HILE the grass was growing tall and rank on Chastelâr's grave, the beauty that had bewildered and destroyed him was unconsciously sowing dissensions and intrigues in half the Courts of Europe.

Not only on the southern side the Tweed did every turbulent noble and ambitious statesman look to Mary Stuart's marriage as, in one way or other, a stepping-stone to his own aggrandisement, but each of the numerous parties in the state was prepared to put forward and support its candidate for her hand, totally irrespective of the lovely Queen's personal feelings and predilections. Austria, Savoy, Spain, had also their claimants for the desired alliance; and it would be difficult to calculate the multiplicity of schemes and combinations, originating in the desire of possessing the heiress to two kingdoms and the most fascinating woman of the age.

Perhaps the proposed union with the Crown-Prince

of Spain was, of all matrimonial overtures, the most unpopular in Great Britain; and the Protestant party, now completely in the ascendant both in England and Scotland, would have resorted to the strongest measures rather than submit to such an arrangement.

All the engines of an unscrupulous diplomacy were ready to be put in motion for the purpose of thwarting Don Carlos and over-reaching his emissaries. Nor were Elizabeth and her agents likely to be restrained by any over-refinement of delicacy in a matter which concerned the stability of the English Queen's power, and the very existence of her government.

In the meantime, Mary and her Maidens floated, so to speak, on the surface of all this turbulence and vexation, as the sea-bird floats with unruffled plumage on the restless waves. Their life was indeed one of constant variety and adventure, for their royal Mistress was too thorough a Stuart not to identify herself with all the difficulties and troubles of her kingdom, whilst the bonds of affection which rivetted her attendants to her service were but drawn closer every day, by the dangers and hardships they shared in their huntings and progresses and judicial proceedings, through the length and breadth of Scotland.

Nevertheless, winter after winter found them established once more, over their peaceful embroidery, at Holyrood; beautiful and merry and unchanged as ever—all but one.

Mary Hamilton, though she still showed the same unbounded devotion to her Mistress, the same sweetness of disposition towards her companions, was cruelly altered now.

It is very sad to read in any human face the unerring symptoms of a broken heart; to watch the eye sinking, the cheek falling, and the lines about the mouth deepening day by day; to note the listless step, the morbid craving for solitude, the painful shrinking from all that is bright and beautiful,—from a strain of sweet music, a gleam of spring sunshine, or the laugh of a happy child, as the aching eye shrinks from light, and, above all, the dreary smile that seems to protest patiently against the torture, while the sufferer is kind and forgiving still. We are almost tempted to ask, why should there be such sorrow here on earth! But we are satisfied and reassured, recalling a certain pledge that cannot deceive, remembering who it was that declared in mercy and sympathy, 'Blessed are those that mourn, for they shall be comforted.'

Her companions could not fail to notice the change that was thus wasting the very existence of their favourite, and each, in her own way, strove to show her fellow-feeling and her concern. Mary Carmichael was, perhaps, the least demonstrative of the three; but this young lady had of late been extremely engrossed with her own affairs, and seemed to acquire additional hardness of character and reserve of demeanour day by day. Her interviews with the stranger in the Abbey-garden, always clandestine and always affectionate, took place at regular intervals, and she seldom saw Walter Maxwell now, avoiding indeed every occasion of meeting him, and treating him, when they did happen to be together, with a coldness and displeasure which he was the last man on earth to accept with resignation, and which was gradually, but surely, estranging his affection from her altogether. He did not see the longing looks that followed him when his back was turned; he did not hear the sigh that rose so wearily to her lips when she was alone; he only thought her fickle, heartless, ungenerous, and unjust, determined to have nothing more to do with her, felt hurt and angry, yet very much ashamed of himself for entertaining either of these sentiments on her account.

All this time Mr. Randolph had not been idle at the Court of Holyrood, fulfilling his ministering with a tact and energy peculiarly his own, and valued as they deserved by his bustling Mistress and her astute adviser, the celebrated Cecil. Wherever there was an intrigue brewing, the English Ambassador was not to be satisfied until he was at the bottom of it; wherever there was a mystery, he sifted it thoroughly, analysing with diplomatic chemistry its component parts, and amalgamating the whole into a confusion worse confounded when he had done with it.

The many marriage proposals to the Queen kept his hands full, and the contradictory orders he received from his Sovereign, who with all her great qualities, was sufficiently a woman never to be quite sure of her own mind for two consecutive days, by no means tended to simplify or facilitate the duties of his office. Nevertheless he found time to press his suit ardently with Mary Beton, insinuating himself sufficiently into her affections to worm out of her all the intelligence he could possibly obtain, yet with characteristic caution, never failing to stop short of the boundary beyond which he must compromise or embarrass himself. And yet Mr. Randolph with his clever, scheming, well-balanced mind, and his thoroughly disciplined heart, was but human after all; none other was so pleasant to him as this daily duty of making love to Mary Beton; her dignity and her beauty gratified his fastidious taste, and her obvious admiration of himself could not but make an impression on his callous heart.

Sometimes even over him, the hardened man of the world, stole a soft vision of something better than ciphers and protocols and despatches—of pleasant words and loving looks, and little children and a home; but a moment of reflection brushed all such weaknesses from his path, and the perusal of a state-paper from Cecil soon restored him to his philosophy. Then he remembered that in a career like his every stepping-stone to greatness must be prized and used only as such; however fair its polish, however valuable its quality, it must be crushed under his heel to gain a firmer foot-hold, and spurned in turn when done with, for his upward spring to the next. Randolph sought out tools for his own purpose in all directions; when he failed to find an appropriate instrument, he shaped one to his hand for himself.

Now it had not escaped the watchful eyes of mistress Beton that a certain stranger, with whom Mary Carmichael seemed extremely intimate, came and went at stated intervals to and from the Court. With all her vigilance, however, she had never been able to discover the exact object of these frequent visits. Had she been satisfied that it was a simple love-affair, she might indeed on her own responsibility have stifled the whole proceeding by authority; but a hint to that effect hazarded to the Queen had been so coldly received as to convince her that the intrigue, whatever might be its object, was carried on with Mary's cognizance and approval.

More than any of the other maids-of-honour, mistress Carmichael had free liberty to come and go as she chose. On occasion she was closeted secretly with her Mistress; and more than once these private consultations were known to have been preceded or followed by an assignation with the mysterious stranger. Mary Beton could not make it out; she was satisfied that her junior had a lover who was deeply engaged in a political intrigue. She must have been more or less than woman had her curiosity not been aroused and her disapprobation excited. It was a relief to tell Randolph of her suspicions, and a pleasure to listen to the eloquence of his gratitude for the confidence thus reposed in him. In consequence of these disclosures the diplomatist resolved to cultivate a greater familiarity with Maxwell, of whom he had never entirely lost sight, and whose honest nature he doubted not he could mould to his own purposes; the more so that in common with the rest of the Court, he was aware of Walter's feelings towards Mary Carmichael, which the lover believed to be inscrutably hidden in his own heart.

To a cynical disposition it is no small amusement to watch the demeanour of an offended swain. Women, who are hypocrites from the cradle, manage to conceal their feelings creditably enough, and we may take leave to doubt whether these feelings themselves are so engrossing as they would have the other sex believe; but a man, one of the Lords of the Creation, who 'dotes yet

doubts, suspects yet strongly loves,' is an object that
may at least be termed deplorable if not ridiculous.
He always over-acts his part so completely, his affectation of indifference is so transparent, his bearing of
scrupulous courtesy and offended dignity so ludicrous,
and his sudden fits of remorse so unaccountable, that
the world in general contemplates him with comical
surprise, and the object herself regards him with secret
triumph and outward contempt.

'Treat a woman frankly,' quoth Lovelace, in his
treatise on this difficult topic, ' and, strange as it may
at first sight appear, like a rational creature. This
course is sure to produce a misunderstanding; but
remember, the sooner there is a trial of strength the
better. Afterwards, if you cannot preserve a *bonâ
fide* and complete indifference, take care to absent
yourself from the subject under treatment. It is indispensable never to appear at a disadvantage. If
elsewhere, the subject, whose imagination is vivid, will
picture you as more pleasingly employed than in its
society. This rouses emulation and stimulates self-esteem, of both which qualities it possesses a large
share. When it is satisfied you can do perfectly well
without it, if it has the slightest inclination to be
tamed, it will come to the hand of its own accord; if
it has not, all your pains are but labour thrown away,
and only render you less fitted to cope with such other
subjects of the species as it may seem desirable to
reduce to obedience. Always remember this, that the
men whom women love best are those over whom they
have the least influence, and of whom they stand somewhat in awe.'

Is Lovelace right? We have quoted from memory, but such is the gist of his theory, the truth of which our own observation of such matters would lead us to concede; the difficulty seems to be in reducing it to practice. The generous nature is more willing to give than to receive, and takes all the shame and all the suffering ungrudgingly on its own shoulders.

'Malo cum Platone errare.'

It may be better to fail thus, than to triumph with Lovelace.

Walter Maxwell was proud, lonely, and unhappy. It was under these circumstances that master Randolph bade him to dinner in his lodging at twelve o'clock noon, and studiously avoided asking any other guest to meet him.

The refined taste of the Englishman had gathered about him even in the northern capital every luxury of which the age admitted. Good living and diplomacy have ever gone together, from the roast mutton consumed in council before Troy to the Nesselrode puddings of to-day.

Honest Jenkin, an invaluable domestic, received his master's guest with a grin of recognition. He had not forgotten their night skirmish on the Border some two years ago, and after the manner of his kind had assumed a vested interest in Maxwell for the rest of his life.

'Master Randolph was in his closet concluding a despatch,' he said, placing a seat for the visitor in the chimney-corner. 'The soup would be on the table in five minutes, would master Maxwell divert himself

in the mean time with examining these silver-mounted
dags. They were pretty pistolets enough. We would
have been none the worse of them that moonlight night
in the "Debateable Land."'

Maxwell smiled, and whilst Jenkin bustled to and
fro about his hospitable labours, warmed himself at
the wood-fire and took a survey of the Ambassador's
apartment.

It presented the same medley of refinement and sim-
plicity, of comfort and contrivance, which may be observed in an officer's barrack-room of the present day.
Sundry mails and leather trunks, all adapted for
carriage on horseback, were converted into cases for
books and writings, and otherwise served temporary
purposes for which they were not intended. The
massive oaken chairs and tables, rough primitive fur-
niture belonging to the mansion, were covered by skins
and shawls of considerable value, Randolph's own property, and presented to him at different times by the
great personages with whom he came in contact. Costly
arms of beautiful workmanship, richly-chased drinking
vessels and elaborate ornaments of great value in small
compass, that had come into his possession in the same
manner, were scattered about the apartment. A sword
of the finest temper Italian forges could produce, inlaid
with gold and ornamented with precious stones, the
gift of the Duke of Savoy, lay carelessly on a writing-
table across a Bible printed at Geneva, as the in-
scription on its leather cover attested, for Mr. Randolph's especial acceptance; and propped against the
hilt of this beautiful weapon smiled a miniature portrait
of Elizabeth, with tightly-curling yellow hair, set pro-

fusely in diamonds. Quantities of papers and memoranda, none, we may be sure, of the slightest importance, littered the floor; a pair of spurs, a hawking-glove with a set of jesses and a lure were on the high chimney-piece grouped about the beautiful cup that the Queen of Scotland had herself bestowed on the Minister; whilst ranged in a semi-circle before the fire, ripening and mellowing in its comfortable glow, stood a row of tapering flasks, blushing with the goodly vintage of Bordeaux. As Jenkin appeared with the dinner at one door, Randolph came forward with his open pleasant manner to meet his guest through another.

'Work is done for to-day!' exclaimed the diplomatist, with the bright air of a boy released from school. 'Master Maxwell, you are heartily welcome, once for all. Be seated, I pray you. Were a despatch to arrive post from my gracious Mistress herself, I should thrust it aside like the noble Roman, fill me a cup of wine, as I do now, to your health, and say, "Business to-morrow!"'

'No man has so good a right to leisure as yourself,' replied his guest doing as he was bid, and returning the pledge in a hearty draught, 'for no man gets through so much work in so short a time. Even Maitland, who is our most accomplished pen-man here in the North, vows that he cannot but marvel at the dispatch with which the English affairs are conducted.'

'It is all plain-sailing,' replied Randolph, with an appearance of the most engaging candour. 'My instructions are usually so intelligible and above-board, that I have but to act on them without delay. Frankly, my friend, between you and me, the only complications

I have are owing to the mystery that is kept up about your Queen's marriage. But this is no time for business. Fill your cup once more. Honest Jenkin's catering requires to be washed down with good wine. The fare is moderate enough, but at least I can answer for the liquor.'

Both by precept and example Randolph encouraged his guest to do justice to his hospitality, and led the conversation, as he well knew how, to such topics as he thought would most interest a man of his companion's age and habits. Horses, hawks, and hounds, wine, women, the latest gossip at Holyrood, the newest jest from the French Court, and the recent improvements in warlike arms and tactics, such were the subjects lightly touched upon in turn, and each was made the reason or the excuse for a fresh bumper; but all the while the diplomatist's attention was never taken off the object he had in view. Like some skilful chemist, he watched the gradual fusion of his materials and waited patiently for the moment of projection. It did not escape him, however, that Maxwell was preoccupied and out of spirits, that though he bore his share in the dialogue courteously enough, it was with an obvious effort, and that every fresh cup he emptied seemed rather to drown, than to cherish, the few sparks of hilarity which he had shown at the commencement of the entertainment.

At a sign from his master, Jenkin set a flask of rich Cyprus wine on the table, and Randolph, dismissing the domestic, heaped fresh logs upon the fire, and drew his chair towards his guest, as if he were growing exceedingly confidential and communicative.

'Are you for the revels at the Palace to-night?' said he, with a meaning look at the bravery of Walter's attire. 'We may as well go together. In the mean time (we are old friends, good master Maxwell), I have something to say to you. Of course in the strictest confidence.'

'Of course,' replied Maxwell, with rather a disturbed expression of countenance, which subsided, however, almost immediately into his usual steady composure.

The Ambassador filled his guest's cup and his own.

'You and I are interested in the same matter,' said he, not entirely repressing his habitual cynicism, 'and such a community forms the strongest bond of friendship. If I can prove to you that by helping me you benefit yourself, can I count upon your assistance?'

'You must explain your meaning more clearly,' replied the other, with something of contempt in his tone. 'Remember, I am a soldier, and no diplomatist.'

'You are a soldier, I know,' rejoined Randolph, 'and a brave one. You are loyal and generous and true. Mr. Maxwell, I will be frank with you. There is an evil influence at work here, which I think you have the power to crush. Listen. Would you stand by and see your Queen deceived and trifled with by a political cabal, of which the principal emissary is blackening and destroying a reputation that I believe is dearer to you than your own?'

'What mean you?' exclaimed Maxwell, with forced composure, but putting so strong a constraint upon himself that the silver goblet he grasped was dinted by the pressure of his fingers.

'It is no secret now,' answered the other gravely. 'Courtiers' tongues wag freely enough on such subjects, and you must not be wrath with me for repeating in your own behalf simply what I hear. It is well known that mistress Carmichael, beautiful mistress Carmichael, cold mistress Carmichael, proud mistress Carmichael,' (he watched the effect of each epithet in succession on his irritated listener,) 'has taken to herself a friend, an admirer, a lover, call it what you will, with whom she holds clandestine interviews in the Abbey-garden at night. As I live, 'tis the common talk of the Palace; and people laugh and whisper and sneer about the spotless Maries, and wonder why the Queen takes no notice of it. Nay, chafe not with *me*. In good faith, man, I do but tell you this as a friend. I have little enough to do with ladies, you know.'

'And what is all this to me?' asked Maxwell, with such admirable self-command that Randolph could not help thinking what a pity it was he did not follow out the profession of state-craft. Nevertheless, every word had struck home, and although his voice was so steady and his face so calm, the perspiration stood on his brow, and there was a dangerous glitter in his deep-set eyes.

'Why, thus much,' returned Randolph; 'that had this intriguer, whoever he may be, no claims but his own merit to the notice of Mary Carmichael, I believe, and those who know her best affirm, that she would never have condescended to notice him. But these interviews, granted for some hidden purpose unconnected with gallantry, are compromising her till she is gradually falling into his power, and the poor girl will find herself at last compelled to accept as a lover the man for whom she does *not* care, unless she be extricated from her false position by the man for whom she *does*.'

'Meaning me,' said Maxwell, looking steadily in the Minister's face.

'Meaning you,' replied the latter, continuing in the most friendly tone; 'you have the right, it seems to me, and you ought to have the will to unmask this intruder. It is your own fault, Maxwell, with good friends at your back, if you have not the power. Come, you may count upon me for one in this matter. To-night I have reason to believe mistress Carmichael will again meet this mysterious personage in the Abbey-garden, whilst the revel is at high tide in the Palace. Follow her to the tryst, confront your rival and compel him to declare himself or to do you reason with his sword. If needed I will be at your back, and should all other means fail, six inches of cold steel can easily square accounts between you.'

'And your reason for thus interesting yourself in my concerns?' demanded Maxwell, with a dry laugh. 'Is it purely out of friendship for me, master Randolph?'

'Now you speak like a sensible man,' replied the diplomatist, 'and I answer you with the frankness you deserve. No! with all my regard for you, this interest, on my part, is *not* entirely for your sake. I have reason to mistrust this stranger; I have my suspicions of some dark plot, against which it is my bounden duty to be on my guard. If he be a friend, my plan will at once set matters on a proper footing, both as regards yourself and the lady of whom we speak. If an enemy, the sooner he is removed from our path the better.

Have I not convinced you that our interests are identical? The day wanes; one more cup of the Cyprus, master Maxwell, and then, first to the Palace, afterwards to the garden.'

Maxwell filled and emptied the cup of Cyprus as he was bidden; but his was a temperament on which wine took but little effect, or rather, in which it stimulated the faculties without upsetting the judgment. Even Randolph's brain, powerful as that organ undoubtedly was, could not have been less affected by his potations than was the soldier's.

As the pair, ostensibly dismissing the subject from their minds, talked gaily on about other matters, it would have been amusing to note the dexterity with which the diplomatist adapted his conversation to the purpose he had in view. How, with a casual remark here, a covert sarcasm there, he endeavoured to stimulate the other's jealousy and to rouse his alarm, whilst, at the same time, with many a plausible argument and choice anecdote, introduced as it were by chance, he endeavoured to establish the expediency of prompt and desperate measures on all occasions where a man had to deal with cases of mystery and intrigue.

Maxwell listened attentively, but the inscrutable repose of his countenance baffled even Randolph's penetration, and he contented himself with vague and general replies, of which the other could make nothing. Nevertheless he was resolving in his own mind what to do. With all his exterior of adamant he was sufficiently vulnerable within. Bitterly hurt and offended at Mary Carmichael's conduct, he had determined to forget her, but the old wound was only superficially healed over, and it would not bear being touched or tampered with yet. Also his attachment to that young lady had been of the purest and most unselfish order, and such an affection never fails to evoke all the latent generosity of a noble heart. His own impulse, as a gentleman, was to give his rival every fair advantage, to treat him, at least, as an open and honourable foe ; to warn him that his movements were watched and his personal safety endangered ; and to tell him, point blank, that he had done this for the sake of her whom they both loved. Surely such frankness would meet with the return it deserved, and then if Mary really preferred this stranger, why, the dream was over, that was all Any privation was better than this continual uncertainty; it was but giving her up, and the world would be before him again,—something whispered that it would be a very different world, nevertheless. However, he made up his mind, and was more than usually merry with Randolph as they proceeded together towards Holyrood.

CHAPTER XXVI.

'I leant my back into an aik,
    I thought it was a trusty tree,
But first it bowed and syne it brak'
    Sae my true love did lightly me.

'O waly, waly—gin love be bonny
    A little time while it is new,
But when it's auld, it waxeth cauld,
    And fades away like morning dew.'

T was the anniversary of Twelfth-night, and the Feast of the Bean was in act of celebration with great glee and splendour when the English Minister and his companion entered the reception-rooms of the Palace. This favourite pastime, borrowed from the Court of France, has come down to us in modern days under the form of 'drawing for king and queen;' the bean was concealed in the twelfth cake, and the dame to whose share it fell was chosen with much mock solemnity as queen of the night. On the present occasion the lot had fallen to Mary Beton, and her indulgent Mistress, with that playful good-humour which so endeared her to her attendants, had insisted on decking the leader of the revels with the most splendid attire her own royal wardrobe contained.

In case that any lady should condescend to look into

the dry pages of a historical novel, we will endeavour to the extent of our poor abilities to present the details of a '*grande toilette*' of the fifteenth century.

A sweeping robe of cloth of silver, heavy with embroidery and ornamented with medallions of pearls down the front of the dress, which was looped backwards at the knee and fastened with bunches of red and white roses, disclosing a petticoat of white silk damask, long and ample so as to cover the feet encased in their satin shoes; at the waist a girdle of precious stones arched over the hips, and coming downwards to a point in front, marked the outline of the figure; while a collar of sapphires and rubies close round the neck lurked and sparkled under the clouds of scalloped lace that composed the ruff; the sleeves of the gown open at the elbow, terminated in ruffles of the lightest gauze, and thick gold bracelets on the wrists; the hair gathered into heavy masses at the back of the head was dragged somewhat off the temples, so as to show the delicate ears with their glittering ear-rings; whilst over the whole figure, relieving its dazzling whiteness, was thrown a satin mantle or scarf of *cramoisie*, the well-known deep rich hue, something between crimson and plum-colour, which was such a favourite with the elaborate *coquettes* of that sumptuous period.

Thus attired, majestic Mary Beton looked every inch a queen, and had it not been for the presence of her Mistress simply dressed in her usual mourning garb, yet 'beautiful exceedingly' where all were beautiful, the maid-of-honour would have rivetted every eye on her magnificent exterior. Randolph felt a thrill of triumph and gratification when she caught his attention, something akin perhaps to that which is experienced by the wary deer-stalker while he contemplates the royal stag with his branching antlers, the pride of the forest, within point-blank range of his rifle. The Ambassador, however, had but little time to admire, for the Queen called him to her with such marked favour immediately on his entrance, that he felt convinced something of more importance than usual was in the wind, and resolved from whatever quarter it blew, that at least it should not throw any dust in *his* eyes.

After receiving very graciously the compliments which Mr. Randolph proffered on the splendour of the entertainment, Mary darted at him a keen glance of mingled watchfulness and amusement, then observed carelessly,

'What think ye of this chamber for a real King and Queen to hold their state in, master Randolph? Since it hath been newly decorated, methinks a King-Consort might be satisfied with his lodging. Ere another Twelfth-night comes round, the lot may have fallen, who knows? and these faithful damsels of mine may have been released from their vow.'

He stole a look at Mary Beton surrounded by her mock courtiers and immersed in the game of forfeits which they were all playing with the eagerness of children, and wondered whether he would like to marry her or not; but he answered the Queen as if the subject she had broached, so far from being unexpected, had occupied his attention for days.

'Your Majesty anticipates the congratulations I am but waiting an opportunity to offer. May I give my own Mistress joy on your acceding so cordially to her views for your welfare?'

'You may do what you have authority for, and no more,' replied the Queen severely. 'My Cousin can scarce spare me that Master of the Horse of hers whom she so much regardeth herself, nor am I so scantily supplied with suitors that I need trespass on her generosity for so precious a bridegroom. Come, Mr. Randolph,' she added gaily, ' this is Twelfth-night, and we read riddles and play at forfeits. Can you not read me mine?'

'Your Grace must condescend to instruct me,' replied he, running over his information and calculating probabilities with inconceivable rapidity in his own mind; also studiously abstaining from the guess he thought most likely to hit the mark. ' Where the prize is of such value all are so unworthy that it reduces the competitors to a level. I can aim no nearer the white than my first shaft, your Grace. A suitor for such a hand as yours should have some weighty influence to back him, in addition to unbounded merits of his own.'

'You seem to have considered the subject deeply,' said the Queen, laughing. ' Come, Mr. Randolph, for very pastime let us hear the qualifications you deem indispensable to an admirer of Mary Stuart.'

He paused for an instant, enumerating in his own mind the different qualities of the nobleman whom he was instructed, at least ostensibly, to put forward, and then proceeded with an air of the utmost deference and humility,

' He should be a gentleman of admirable presence; of skill in courtly exercises; of varied accomplishments; familiar with the customs of palaces; brave, noble, and learned: he should be of no foreign extraction, neither

Frenchman, Spaniard, nor Italian; suitable in point of years, of language, and of country.'

She nodded archly every time he paused in his catalogue, then added, with an enquiring look,

'And of royal lineage as well? Surely like pairs with like, and a Stuart should only mate with a Stuart.'

It was a home thrust. It corroborated much that he had already suspected, and explained a good deal that had sufficiently puzzled even Randolph, but he never winced or started; to judge by his face it was the communication, of all others, for which he was best prepared, and whilst he ran over, as quick as thought, the different combinations to which such a projected alliance might give rise, and already, in his mind's eye, saw the young Lord Darnley, the suitor to whom Mary alluded, helpless in his toils, he bowed humbly to the Queen and begged her to accept his heart-felt congratulations that she had made her choice at last.

Mary laughed more than ever.

'Not so fast,' said she, 'not so fast. I am discussing possibilities, master Randolph, and you are accepting them for certainties; but enough of this—amusement is our chief business to-night. See, the Queen of the Revels is looking anxiously this way, and you have not been to pay her your homage yet. Delay no longer, her displeasure to-night is far weightier and more implacable than mine.'

As she spoke she dismissed him with a courteous gesture, and Randolph, nothing loth, commenced paying his court most assiduously to Mary Beton, with the double object of spending his time agreeably and worming out of her, ere the night was past, some corroboration of the Queen's vague hints as to her approaching marriage.

It was with secret pride and exultation the Twelfth-night Queen, in all her assumed splendour, beheld the Ambassador approach the circle that formed her sham Court. It would be too much to say that Mary Beton was deeply in love with Randolph, but she experienced from his attentions certain agreeable feelings, that originated in gratified vanity and a sense of her own superiority to her companions. It was indeed no petty triumph to have secured the homage of the fastidious and cynical Thomas Randolph; the man who was the type of refinement and the incarnation of selfishness, avowedly a despiser of women and a free-thinker in love. The pleasure, too, was doubtless in no small degree enhanced by the care-worn face of Alexander Ogilvy, who continued to haunt the Court, with a hopeless perseverance truly edifying, and made himself miserable with the self-immolating regularity peculiar to a lover, and totally inexplicable on any grounds of reason or expediency.

Mary Beton had no objection in the world; she liked to have two strings to her bow. Two! Where is the woman who would refuse half-a-dozen? With all their vanity and all their libertinism, thus much we may safely say in favour of the ruder sex,—a man is usually indisposed to have more than one attachment on his hands at a time. He may behave ungratefully, unfeelingly, brutally, to Dora, but it is for the sake of Flora. For however short a period it may be, yet, *while* he wears those colours, Nora, looking out for prey in every direction, shall strive to fascinate him in vain. But how different is the conduct of the last named personage: brilliant and seductive, it is no reason because she is herself in love with Tom, that she should refrain from the massacre of Jack, Dick, and Harry; nay, if Bill be fortunate enough to spend an hour or two in her company, away with him to the shambles too! Shall we pity Nora so very much when she wears the willow for the faithless Tom, and finds out too late that she never really cared a pin for the other victims who, more or less damaged, have made their escape from the toils.

The wrongs of the sexes towards each other are of the cruellest, and it is generous and manly that our sympathy should be given to the weaker portion, but the injuries are not all one way. Many a rugged face is only so grave and stern because it *dare* not, quivering there behind its iron mask, lose for one instant its self-command; many a kindly heart has turned to gall, many an honest nature been warped irrevocably to evil, because the pride of manhood forbids it to ask for that relief which never comes unsought; of course it serves them right; of course we do not pity them; but are they the less lost on that account?

It would have moved even a courtier to witness the expression of sharp pain that swept over Ogilvy's face when Randolph led Mary Beton out to dance, but it was gone in a moment and nobody detected it save the fair cause herself, who moved, we may be sure, all the more proudly through the measure in consequence, and listened, well-pleased as ever, to the mingled honey and vinegar of the Ambassador's flatteries and sarcasms.

Meanwhile the Queen followed by her other maidens glided through the throng, dispensing her notice graciously to all her guests, and more especially those whom she had reason to consider somewhat wavering in their loyalty—a distinction not lost upon Mary Seton, who whispered to her companion,

'This would be a fine time for poor Bothwell now to come back again; see, my dear, even Lord Ruthven has had soft words and kind looks to-night.'

To which the lady addressed, no other than Mary Carmichael, only answered by a smothered sigh, for that nobleman was popularly believed to tamper with the Black Art, and to be an especial adept in the compounding of charms and potions both for friend and foe. She was thinking how delightful it would be to have one of his specific love-philters to do what she liked with, and to whom she would give it. Certainly not to the stranger in the Abbey-garden, he loved her quite well enough already.

Somehow at this moment her eye sought out the figure of Walter Maxwell, who was standing apart in the recess of one of the windows, and looking at her with a kind of pitying sadness, as men do on an object once dearly prized which they will never see again. It was so unusual now for them to exchange glances, much less words, that the sight troubled her; she turned red first and then very pale. He stirred and made a step forward as if to advance and speak to her, but seeming to think better of it, crossed his arms upon his breast and resumed his former position. Following the Queen she was obliged to pass very near him, and lowering her eyes to avoid meeting his glance, she was distressed and ashamed to find that they were full of tears.

There is a mysterious kind of sympathy often existing between those who have some common cause of suffering. Two gouty old gentlemen are never tired of detailing to each other their respective symptoms of *podagra*; and weak-minded ladies subject to 'nervous attacks' have been overheard to interchange the most surprising confidences regarding that remarkable ailment; in the same manner a couple of lovers, not a *pair*, are drawn towards each other by a community of sorrow.

Alexander Ogilvy took his place by Mary Carmichael's side, and sought in that lady's blue eyes at least commiseration for his sorrows. Placing a chair for her a little out of the crowd, he conversed with her on the heat of the room, the beauty of the dresses, her own successful toilet, and such light topics, gradually lowering his voice and bringing the conversation round to the subject nearest his heart.

'A bird hath whispered in my ear,' said he, 'that we must look ere long to have a king-consort at Holyrood. The Maries are more interested in the matter than the whole of Scotland beside. You will be freed from your vow; choose each of you a mate and pair off like the fowls of the air ere another St. Valentine be past. What say you, mistress Carmichael, sings my little bird true or false? I am no courtier you know.'

'And yet you are much at Court,' she answered absently, 'particularly of late, master Ogilvy; it was but yesterday the Queen pointing you out to Mary Beton, commended the bravery of your attire.'

Ogilvy coloured, looking very much alarmed yet not altogether displeased.

'And what said mistress Beton?' he asked anxiously.

His discomposure was so obvious that it was well for him he had not to do with mischievous Mary Seton or even with his present companion had she been in other than a subdued and melancholy frame of mind. In most women the temptation to mockery would have been irresistible, but mistress Carmichael only replied carelessly,

'That you were the properest man at Holyrood, and that she thought our gallants of the Court wore the French air more naturally than did the Southrons.'

'Did she *really* say so?' he exclaimed eagerly; 'and do you believe she meant it? You know her well, mistress Carmichael; is it not true that she is herself too irresistibly attracted towards the Southron? Do you not think that when hood and jesses are fairly doffed once for all, she will fly her pitch toward the Border, aye, and strike her quarry far on the southern side?'

Mary Carmichael followed the direction of his glance to where mistress Beton stood radiant in her Twelfth-night bravery, and listening with a heightened colour and a well-pleased air to Randolph's flatteries; but she pitied whilst she marked the suffering that was too apparent in her questioner's gaze, and replied gently to his thoughts rather than his words,

'Gratified vanity is one thing, and real preference another. A woman oft-times likes that suitor best whom most she seems to avoid. Perhaps for that very reason; perhaps because she is weak at heart and cannot help herself.'

She spoke the last sentence low, and more to herself than to him. She was willing to console him, for the deeper a kind nature is wounded, the more it feels for the sorrows of others. Also, it may be that she found a certain relief in repeating the lesson it had cost her so much pains to learn.

He drew closer to her.

'Thank you,' said he, with a beaming look of gratitude. 'You are a true friend! Believe me, mistress Carmichael, I am not ungrateful. Can I serve you in any way in return?'

'It is no question of that,' she replied. 'Our positions are so different. I only say to you, remember your own motto, "To the End." If I were a man I think I could trust and hope for ever. I think I could be staunch and unselfish and true, in defiance of sorrow, suffering, opposition, nay even of ingratitude and neglect. I would prove to the woman whom I had chosen that at least she must be proud of my choice, that a man's honest affection was no vacillating fancy, but an eternal truth; and even if she did not love me I would force her to confess that it was her own inferiority of nature that could not mate with mine. But why should I talk thus to you?' she added, breaking off with rather a bitter laugh, 'You are a *man;* you cannot understand me; you will not believe in anything unless you can see it with your two eyes, and grasp it in your two hands, and be told by all your friends besides, that it is there. If you had but one gold piece in the world you must beat it out thin, and lacker it over your spurs, and your housings, and the hilt of your sword; you could not hide it away in your bosom and keep it unspent and unsuspected next your heart!'

'I know not,' he said, with a brightening face; 'your words give me hope. I seem to see things differently since you have been speaking to me. You are my good angel. Help me; advise me; tell me what I had better do.'

'In the first place go and talk to somebody else,' she replied, laughing. 'You will scarcely advance the cause you have at heart by whispering with me in a corner. Looks of enquiry if not displeasure have been already shot this way, and although, perhaps, we are the only two people in this room who never could be more than friends, courtiers' eyes are so sharp and their inferences so good-natured, that they have probably ere this made their usual grand discovery of that which does not exist. And so, good master Ogilvy, my last word is, think of your motto, and speed you well!'

Thus speaking she made him a stately curtsey and withdrew towards the Queen, but Mary Carmichael was right, and their interview, short as it was, had been remarked by more than one interested observer.

Though it costs the animal many stripes and much vexation doubtless to acquire the accomplishment, we have seen a dog so well broke as to forego at his owner's word a tempting morsel placed within his reach, licking his lips indeed and looking longingly after it, yet exhibiting, nevertheless, a noble mastery over his inclinations. But let another dog come by and snatch the bone thus ceded to a sense of duty, and all his self-restraint vanishes on the instant. Open-mouthed he rushes to wrest it from the intruder, and that which but a moment ago was an advantage he could philosophically resign, becomes immediately a necessity that he will break through all bounds to attain. So is it with mankind. We can give up, or rather we fancy we have given up the one bright hope that gilded our existence. We see the dear face that used to make the very sunshine of our heart altered and estranged, perhaps cold and distant, perhaps turned scornfully away. We think we can bear our burden resignedly enough. There is a great blank in our lives, felt less in time of sorrow than at those seasons when, were it not for our loss, we think we should be so contented, so happy. There is a sense of desolation, a consciousness of old age coming on and being welcome; a morbid inclination to receive adversity with open arms, but yet we man ourselves against the calamity, strong to oppose and constant to endure. We have not felt the sting yet. Whilst we are in the cold shade let the dear face beam upon another; let the tones so cruel now and hard to *us*, fall with the well-remembered cadence on *his* ear; let him be the recipient of the thousand tender cares and winning ways that used to bring tears of affection into our eyes: then and not till then have we sustained the sharpest pain that life has to inflict; then and not till then do we feel that there is no sorrow like to our sorrow, and that it is well for us it is transient from its very nature, or heart and brain would give way under the stroke.

Mary Beton was well satisfied to receive the homage of her English admirer, and, in order to ensure it, was perfectly willing to discard her sincerer suitor. Poor Ogilvy might pine and sigh as he pleased, without gaining so much as a kind word or an approving glance; but this rigorous treatment was only to endure so long as she felt he was her property: the dog's wages were to be given to the dog's honest obedience and fidelity. It was quite a different matter when he appeared to have transferred his allegiance to another. Though she did not like him well enough to give up Randolph for his sake, she had no idea of losing him altogether. Even if she had no use for him, he had no right to belong to any one else, and it was with far more of anxiety and concern than usually overspread those calm features, that mistress Beton glanced continually towards the corner where he was whispering with Mary Carmichael, while she listened to the smooth phrases of the English Ambassador with an absent air and a forced smile.

Nor was the stately maid-of-honour the only person in that noble assemblage who felt acutely the difference between the active and passive moods of the verb 'to give up.' Walter Maxwell, hurt, jealous, and indignant, had for long accustomed himself to look upon Mary Carmichael as one who was dead to him for evermore; had trained himself to meet her coldly and calmly when their respective duties brought them unavoidably together, and to shun her on all other occasions with scrupulous self-denial; nay, was beginning to find a certain gloomy satisfaction in the violence he was capable of doing to his own feelings, and a certain savage triumph in the reflection that he, too, could be as unkind and heartless and indifferent as a woman! But when he saw her thus engrossed with Ogilvy's conversation, evidently of a mysterious and interesting nature; when he marked, as he did at a glance, the softened expression of her face and the wistful tenderness in her blue eyes, he experienced a sensation of pain once more, to which he had thought he was henceforth to be a stranger, and felt again for an instant as he had felt that well remembered night, when he came upon her so unexpectedly at her tryst in the Abbey-garden.

The same cause produces strangely different effects upon different individuals. Whilst Mary Beton, under the influence of jealousy, was becoming restless, captious, and even irritable (much, it must be confessed, to the secret amusement of Mr. Thomas Randolph), Walter Maxwell felt a fresh impulse given to that generosity, which prompted him to put an end to-night to his anxieties and misgivings once for all.

The Queen, in the meantime, seeking, in her innocence and gaiety of heart, to keep up the characteristic merriment of the feast, was unconsciously exciting the displeasure of her nobility, and unwittingly preparing the downfall of her versatile little favourite—the Italian, Riccio.

Disregarding the coarser witticisms and grotesque antics of James Geddes, who indeed had become a duller fool day by day since the shock his feeble intellects sustained on the morning of Chastelâr's death, Mary had summoned her private secretary into the centre of the illustrious circle which surrounded her, and, with a familiarity exceedingly displeasing to the haughty Scottish barons, bade him *improvise*, after the manner of his country, for their amusement. Nothing daunted by bent brows and scornful looks, the glib foreigner, placing himself on a cushion at the Queen's feet, commenced a lively tale, of which the incidents and the language, for it was related in French, were most displeasing to his audience. It turned upon one of those fables so popular at the time in Italy, and was, indeed, both in its details and its catastrophe, especially unsuitable to the practical nature and affected asceticism of the Scottish character at that period.

'There was a beautiful flower,' said he, his little black eyes twinkling at the Queen while he spoke, 'growing in a fair garden through which ran a mountain stream, and the birds of the air and the insects of the noontide came to pay their court to this flower and to win a breath of her fragrance, for she was the pride of all earthly plants and the queen of the garden. So the humming bird flitted by in his bravery, and she marked not his liveries of blue and gold, nor bent her head towards him, but let him pass on to court the flowers of his own tropical land, gorgeous without perfume, dazzling but loveless, like a fair woman without a heart. And the nightingale sang his life away to please her, and, wooing her with his last notes, died hungering when the evening star shone out above the trees. Then the butterfly brought his painted coat and his gay manners and fluttered about her, making sure that a courtier like himself must prevail; but she bent not her head nor moved one of her leaves towards him, though the breeze was sighing softly around her and shaking the dewdrops from her stem.

'None of the gay and gaudy seemed to win the favour of that queenly flower. At length a bee came buzzing home from his labours, laden with the honey-dew that he had been gathering far and wide. He thought to rest on her petals and distil fresh treasures from her chalice, but she shook her beautiful blossoms merrily in the breeze and waved him scornfully away.

'All the birds of the air and the noon-tide insects marvelled that she would have none of them, for they deemed her haughty and unsociable, whispering to one another of the pride that goeth before a fall.

'Now, even as she shook her petals in disdain, she opened her heart to the daylight, and at its very core lay concealed a lazy, useless drone. Then the humming-bird and the butterfly and the bee laughed together, for they said,

'Of what avail are beauty and bravery and worth, against possession? And if she have taken the dullest of all insects to her heart, we have but lost our time in suing her, and the nightingale, on the cold earth yonder, hath given his life in vain.'

'There is a moral in my fable, ladies!' added Riccio, with a smile and a shrug of his crooked shoulders,—' a moral that you will all of you acknowledge if you tell truth,—Who shall dictate to a woman's fancy, or reduce to rule the wandering inclinations of a woman's heart!'

The ladies laughed and whispered, some protesting against the conclusion, others pitying the poor nightingale, but all uniting in condemnation of the useless drone.

Lord Ruthven, who had been eyeing the narrator with looks of fierce scorn, strode up to where he was sitting, at the Queen's feet, and asked him in a loud contemptuous voice,

'Were there no WASPS in yonder garden of which you spake, master Tale-teller,—wasps that might give the drone a lesson, and teach him his place was somewhat lower than the bosom of its choicest flower?'

The Italian looked up somewhat scared in his grim questioner's face.

'Nay, signior,' he replied humbly, 'in courtly gardens the wasps must leave their stings behind.'

'Aye! sticking in the carcase of the drone!' returned Ruthven, with a brutal laugh, which was echoed by Morton and one or two other savage-looking noblemen who stood near.

The Queen seemed highly displeased, but true to her conciliatory principle, hastened to change the subject ere these turbulent spirits should further forget their own dignity and the respect due to her presence. Calling her maidens around her, she bade them bring her harp, a beautiful instrument highly ornamented, and proposed it should be the prize of any lady in the company who could sing to it an impromptu measure on a subject she would herself propose.

'I shall play on it no more,' said Mary, with a half-melancholy smile. 'It is only maiden-queens who have time for such follies. A busier day for aught I know, may be about to dawn ere long on Mary Stuart,' (here she cast a sly glance at Randolph, who without seeming to heed her, was listening all attention,) 'and I cannot leave my favourite instrument in better hands than hers who wins it fairly by her skill. Behold! which of you ladies will undertake to strike these strings and improvise a song, as deftly as our little Secretary here has told us a story?'

It was an attempt requiring considerable confidence in such a presence. The ladies gazed on one another in obvious hesitation. Presently a handsome, intellectual-looking woman stepped forward, and curtseying to Her Majesty, bent gracefully without speaking over the instrument.

'Beatrix Gardyn!' exclaimed the Queen with a bright smile, 'the Sappho of the North! I know of none better qualified to do justice to my poor harp; will you begin, Beatrix, at once? Are you waiting for inspiration?'

'The theme, an't please your Majesty?' said Beatrix, bowing her classic head with the utmost composure, and sweeping a masterly prelude over the strings.

The Queen gave another meaning glance at Randolph and laughed again.

'What say you to my marriage? my *possible* marriage, and the consequent release of my four bonny maidens from their celibacy. The subject, methinks, is a noble one, and see, the Maries are listening all attention for your strains.'

Beatrix Gardyn struck a few wandering chords, then with bent brows and kindling eyes fixed on vacancy, broke into a melody to which with but little hesitation and now and then a meaning smile, she adapted the following words:—

THE MAIDENS' VOW.

'A woman may better her word, I trow,
    Now lithe and listen, my lords, to me ;
And I'll tell ye the tale of the Maidens' Vow
    And the roses that bloomed on the bonnie rose tree.

'The Queen of the cluster beyond compare
    Aloft in the pride of her majesty hung,
Bright and beautiful, fresh and fair ;
    The bevy of blossoms around her clung.

'So the winds came wooing from east and west,
    Wooing and whispering frank and free ;
But she folded her petals, quoth she, "I am best
    On a stalk of my own at the top of the tree."

'And they folded their petals, the rose-buds too,
    And closer they clung as the wind swept by,
For they'd vowed a vow that sisterhood true,
    Together to fade and together to die.

'"Never a wind shall a rose-bud wrest,
    Never a gallant shall wile us away,
To wear in his bonnet, to wear on his breast,
    Rose and rose-buds answering, Nay."

'So staunch were the five to their word of mouth,
    That they baffled all suitors who thronged to the bower,
Till a breeze that came murmuring out of the South
    Stole home to the heart of the queenliest flower.

'She drooped in her beauty to hear him sigh,
 And ever the brighter and fairer she grew ;
What wonder then that each rose-bud nigh
 Should open its leaves to the breezes too.

'Oh! gather the dew while the freshness is on,
 Roses and maidens they fade in a day;
Ere you've tasted its sweetness the morning is gone ;
 Love at your leisure but wed while you may.

'Winter is coming and time shall not spare ye,
 Beautiful blossoms so fragrant and sheen ;
Joy to the gallants that win ye and wear ye,
 Joy to the roses, and joy to their queen!'

Rounds of applause followed the conclusion of the song ; the approval with which Mary received it was tantamount to an acknowledgment of its truth, and the courtiers scarce refrained from cheers and such noisy demonstrations of their acquiescence in its purport.

Congratulations were freely tendered to the Maries on their coming release from the vows by which it had long been understood they were bound; and many facetious remarks were directed at those young ladies on a topic which, although next to death the most serious and important in the human destiny, has been considered from time immemorial as a fitting subject for stale witticisms and far-fetched jokes.

In the midst of all this clamour and merriment, Walter Maxwell slipped quietly out of the presence, and when Mary Carmichael, wondering how he would be affected by the news that thus seemed to stir the whole Court, stole a wistful look towards the corner he had lately occupied, behold, he was gone !

After this the buzz of conversation, the rustle of ladies' dresses, the strains of the Queen's musicians, seemed to strike wearily on her ear; how pointless seemed the jests that yet provoked bursts of laughter from the bystanders; how uninteresting the vapid compliments that were yet paid with such an air, and received so graciously; how dull and uninteresting the whole routine of a courtier's life, and the individual items that composed a courtly assemblage. As we must all do sooner or later, for the moment the girl saw life without the varnish, and wondered it had ever looked so bright; she longed for the hour of dismissal when she too had a tryst to keep, a duty to perform. In the mean time we must follow Maxwell into the Abbey-garden.

CHAPTER XXVII.

' The foremost was an aged knight,
  He wore the grey hair on his chin,
Says, " Yield to me thy lady bright,
  An' thou shalt walk the woods within."

' " For me to yield my lady bright
  To such an aged knight as thee,
People wad think I war gane mad,
  Or all the courage flown frae me." '

———

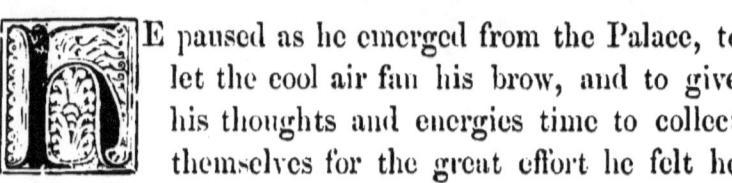E paused as he emerged from the Palace, to let the cool air fan his brow, and to give his thoughts and energies time to collect themselves for the great effort he felt he had to make. Then he walked steadily on to the well-known spot under the apple-tree, where he remembered to have witnessed the interview between Mary Carmichael and her mysterious admirer. Once he had loved that spot so dearly; once he used to linger there for hours together at night, and watch the lights in the apartment inhabited by the Maries; once he was fool enough to feel his heart thrill when *her* shadow crossed the casement. Well! that was all past and gone. It seemed strange the place could be so changed, and yet the same.

There is no feeling so sad as that with which we revisit our earthly paradise, whatever it may be, after our return has been forbidden, and the Angel placed at the gate to warn us off with his flaming sword. Adam and Eve plodded away indeed contentedly into the wilderness, but we, their children, cannot always resign ourselves so philosophically to the inevitable. We plead and pray to be allowed to re-enter, and perhaps to enhance our punishment, the Angel is suffered to give way to our entreaties. Ah! it is the same garden still. Although the trees are lying prostrate, dank, and rotting, on the tufted sward; although the flowers are broken and withered and trampled into the earth; although there are dust and ashes now, and the darkness of desolation, where once the ripe fruit glowed, and the green leaves flickered in the golden floods of noon; yet it is here we first knew paradise; it is from this spot we first caught a glimpse of the dazzling depths of Heaven; it was from that spring, choked and tangled and dried up now, we first drank the waters of life. All is ruined and defiled and destroyed, but it is our Garden of Eden still. We had rather sit here with bowed head and rent garments, than walk the fairest realms of earth, in purple and fine linen, lord and ruler of the whole.

Poor ghosts we are indeed, some of us, even while clothed in our fleshly coverings, and prone to wander to and fro about the spot where we buried our treasures, though they have been dug up and taken away long ago. If we could but sever that cord which links us with the past and cut out the moral gangrene, as we amputate the physical limb when mortification has set in, how healthy would be our spiritual being, how cheerfully we could limp, mutilated but painless, to the grave.

Alas! to some natures it is impossible. To such the punishment of Prometheus is no fiction. The chain and the vulture and the rock must be their portion. Nevertheless they are not eternal, and the Garden of Eden itself, glowing in the summer noon, was but a dreary waste compared with that garden, which men enter by a strait way and through a narrow gate.

Maxwell looked about him with a heavy heart. He was young yet, and the lesson of life which all must learn came painfully to him in the freshness of his youthful hopes.

It takes a long time and a good many reverses to acquire the unenviable stoicism which always *expects* the worst and is seldom disappointed. He was, however, consoled and supported by the consciousness that he had come to a final determination, unselfish and sincere, which would put an end to his doubts once for all. Whilst the dice are yet unthrown, it is a wondrous moral sedative, that resolution to set our whole future on the cast. When they have come up against us, we are by no means satisfied to abide by the issue, but this is an after-consideration, and affects not a whit the vigour of our purpose in the meanwhile.

The watcher had not long to wait. A tall dark figure, cloaked as before, was soon seen gliding to the accustomed spot. Ere he had well reached the apple-tree, Maxwell was already by his side, and had laid his hand upon his shoulder.

The stranger started. Under his cloak a few inches of steel showed themselves out of the scabbard, as his grasp closed upon his sword, but he drove the blade home with a clash, thoroughly re-assured at Maxwell's first sentence.

'I am your friend,' exclaimed the latter hastily, but in a cautious voice, 'at least for the present. You are in danger, and I have come here to warn you.'

There was something so frank in his tones that the other responded immediately. He even lowered the cloak in which his face was muffled and smiled gaily, as he replied,

'I am used to it, my good friend, but equally beholden to you, nevertheless. I would fain know all the same, who you are that take such interest in my welfare, and wherefore. Nay,' he added, more abruptly, 'this is scarcely candid. I know *you*, master Maxwell, and I believe you to be a man of honour and a gentleman; but what you can have to communicate to me is indeed a mystery.'

There was light enough to distinguish the speaker's features. They were those of a singularly handsome man in the prime of life, as his rival did not fail to remark, with a certain defiance and reckless good-humour in their expression. His hair and beard were somewhat grey, but not sufficiently so to destroy the general comeliness of his appearance, and his eyes would have been beautiful even in a woman.

'This is no time to bandy compliments,' answered Maxwell, still in the same low tone. 'You are engaged here in some intrigue; it may or it may not amount to treason. You have been coming and going secretly for months. If you are discovered and arrested, your very life is in danger. Is it not so?'

'Granted,' replied the other, smoothing his grey moustache with a provoking air of calmness. 'There is no game without a hazard. And what then?'

'You have been watched!' urged Maxwell, impatiently. 'You have probably been recognised by those who know you better than I do. Perhaps a few more hours may see you arrested. I tell you Randolph is on your track, that Southron blood-hound who never over-ran a scent nor opened on a false trail. You had better have the devil for your enemy than the English Ambassador!'

'I trust devoutly I may prevail against both,' answered the stranger; then added musingly, 'You say true about Randolph; his schemes are both wide and deep, whilst his hand is as prompt to execute as his brain is subtle to devise. I pray ye, my friend, when did ye learn I was to be here to-night?'

'This day at dinner, and from Randolph himself,' replied Maxwell. 'The Minister spared not the wine-flask I promise you; and had it been any other man I might have believed that he told me more than he intended, but not all the vineyards of the Rhine or the Garonne would influence Randolph's tongue to play false for a syllable to Randolph's brain. Nay, I will deal frankly with you, fair sir. I offered myself to be the means of unmasking you, in order that I might warn you in time and save you from your fate!'

'It was most friendly and considerate,' observed the other with a laugh not far removed from a sneer. 'I would fain know, nevertheless, to what happy chance I am indebted for the interest master Walter Maxwell takes in my preservation. Nay,' he again broke off abruptly, and added with complete sincerity, 'this is unworthy of both of us. You are an honest fellow, master Maxwell, and a loyal gentleman. Roundly now, what is your hidden motive for this proceeding. Come, out with it!'

'My motives are honourable enough,' replied the other, with some difficulty retaining his composure. 'I pray you attribute no hidden meaning to what I have to say. Be frank and open with me, whether friend or foe, as I swear I am frank and open with you.'

'I believe it!' exclaimed the other, extending him his hand; but Maxwell, without taking it, folded his arms across his heart, and proceeded in the low quiet tones of repressed excitement,

'I have no right to assume that your presence here in silence and secrecy is for any other than a political object, and yet from my own knowledge I am satisfied that there are further motives of a private nature. If you feel that what I have done for you to-night deserves any return, I claim your confidence in a matter that is to me one of life and death.'

He wiped the drops from his pale face as he spoke, and the stranger, pitying his obvious agitation, motioned to him courteously to proceed.

'There is a lady of the Court,' resumed Maxwell, still in the same concentrated voice, 'who has allowed herself to hold clandestine interviews with you in this spot by night. No man alive shall make me believe that anything but an ardent and sincere affection would tempt that lady so far to commit herself. Mistress Carmichael is above the weaknesses and petty vanities of her sex. I demand of you, on your honour as a gentleman, to clear her conduct in my eyes by avowing that you are her lover.'

The stranger had started violently when he heard mentioned the proper name of the adventurous damsel whom in truth he was momentarily expecting, but the lower part of his face was again concealed in his cloak, and his whole frame was shaking from some strongly-curbed emotion, while he demanded,

'By what right do you ask so unwarrantable a question?'

'By the right of a pure and holy affection,' answered Maxwell gravely; 'by the right of an unselfish love that would even give her up ungrudgingly to a worthy rival!'

'Hoity-toity, young gentleman!' exclaimed the stranger, breaking forth into an incontrollable fit of laughter, all the more violent that he dared not indulge in it above his breath. 'Thou are not likely to lose aught for lack of asking; thou art one of these wild Iceland falcons, I warrant me, that will fly their pitch, hooded and jessed and all, to strike at every quarry alike. I ought to be angry with thee, man, but I cannot for the life of me. In faith I forgive thee; I forgive thee were it but for the jest's sake.'

He wiped his eyes while he spoke, and turning away stamped upon the ground as he held his sides once more in a convulsion of mirth.

To Maxwell with his feelings wrought up to a pitch of Quixotic generosity, all the more exalted that it was an unusual effort of his practical nature, such a display was irritating in the extreme. It is bad enough to hand over the last stiver you have in your pocket, but when the tears in the recipient's eyes are those of mockery rather than gratitude, it is sufficient to cause an outbreak in the most stoical temperament. The younger man's brow grew dark with passion, and he laid his hand upon his sword.

'At least,' he exclaimed, 'I will force a confession from you; I came here prepared for either alternative. Had you met me frankly and vowed your devotion to her, I would have been your friend for life; if you mean treacherously, I am your rival to the death.'

The other was still laughing.

'Pooh! pooh!' said he carelessly, 'you are meddling with what concerns you not. I thank you for your warning, young sir, and in return I advise you to give up the championship of every dame who comes out with a muffler into the moonlight; I wish you good night, master Maxwell, I would be alone.'

He waved his hand rather contemptuously and turned upon his heel, but Maxwell now boiling with passion placed himself in front of him, and drew his sword.

'You part not thus,' said he; 'by Saint Andrew, I am henceforth your sworn foe. Draw and take your ground if you be a man!'

The other put aside the weapon with his naked hand, and laughed once more. Maxwell's face was white with anger, and his eyes flashed fire. Quick as thought he struck his enemy a smart blow across the shoulder with the flat of his sword.

The smile on the stranger's countenance deepened into a very dangerous expression.

'Nay,' said he in a hissing whisper between his

teeth, 'a wilful man never yet wanted woe; ye have forced me to lug out, youngster, and it shall be to some purpose, I promise ye.'

With that he placed himself on guard with an ominously steady eye, and a hand that, as he bore against his blade, Maxwell quickly discovered to be as skilful as his own.

The wicked steel twined and glittered in the moonlight. As they warmed to their work each man grew more eager and more deadly in the murderous game; thrust and parry, give and take, delicate feint and desperate return were rapidly and breathlessly exchanged, but at the end of a few passes, though neither had gained any advantage, Maxwell's youth and activity began to tell upon his elder antagonist. Already the stranger's brow was covered with sweat, and his breath came quick and short as he traversed here and there, and began perceptibly to give ground. With the true instinct of a swordsman, Maxwell pressed him vigorously when he began to fail, and was in the act of delivering a long meditated and particularly fatal thrust, when he suddenly found his own blade encumbered with a woollen plaid that had been thrown over it, and himself at the mercy of his antagonist. Looking wildly up, he could scarcely believe his eyes when he saw Mary Carmichael's pale face frowning angrily on him, while she clung fondly and imploringly on the stranger's sword-arm, effectually preventing the latter from availing himself, even were he so minded, of the diversion she had so made.

Stunned and stupefied, with his mouth open and his sword-point resting on the ground, Maxwell stood like a man in a dream. Presently his face contracted with an expression of intense pain as he saw Mary once more enveloped in his rival's embrace, and heard her incoherent expressions of tenderness and alarm.

The stranger was soothing her gently and lovingly as a burst of weeping succeeded the effort she had made for his preservation. After a while he turned to his late antagonist, and said,

'You are satisfied now, sir, I presume, and have no wish to renew this foolish and untimely brawl.'

But Maxwell never heard him; with pale face and parted lips, his eyes were still rivetted on Mary Carmichael. He advanced a step towards her, trembling in every limb.

'You love him then?' said he quite gently, but his voice was so changed that the stranger started and turned round thinking some intruder had disturbed them.

'I do! I do!' replied the girl hysterically, still hiding her face on the breast to which she clung.

Maxwell smiled—such a dreary, hopeless smile! then sheathing his sword, turned and walked slowly towards the Palace without another word.

CHAPTER XXVIII.

'I send him the rings from my white fingers,
  The garlands aff my hair;
I send him the heart that's in my breast;
  What would my love hae mair?
And at the fourth kirk in fair Scotland,
  Ye'll bid him meet me there.'

HE little crooked Secretary had been educated in an atmosphere of political agitation and intrigue. To his native Italian shrewdness David Riccio added that quickness of perception, that power of reading men's characters at a glance, which can only be acquired by those who are compelled, amidst the storms through which they guide their bark, to watch every aspect of the horizon, to press every instrument into their service, and take every advantage that shall enable them to weather the gale.

During the Feast of the Bean, whilst the majority of the courtiers were but intent on the merriment of the moment, whilst ladies sipped flattery and lords quaffed wine, it had not escaped the notice of a pair of black southern eyes that Maxwell seemed unusually restless and unhappy; that, in spite of his outward composure, there was something wild and defiant in his glance ; nay, that he wore the look of a man in the right mood for a desperate undertaking—one to whom a dangerous enterprise would appear in the light of a relief.

Either purposely or by chance, Maxwell, returning giddy and half-stupefied from the Abbey-garden, found himself confronted in one of the galleries of the Palace by Her Majesty's private Secretary. The revel was dying gradually out; most of the ladies, following the example of their Sovereign, had retired, and but a few staunch wassailers were left, collected round the buffets and tables, at which wine was still flowing with a lavish hospitality more regal, perhaps, than judicious.

The Secretary (though he had to rise on tip-toe to do it) clapped the soldier familiarly on the back.

'Not to bed, master Maxwell,' he exclaimed in jovial tones, ' not yet to bed, without one cup of sack to wash the night air out of thy throat and wet the wings of sleep, as we say in Italy, so that she cannot choose but fold them around thine head.'

While he spoke he desired one of the Queen's cellarers, who was passing at the moment, to pour him out a measure of the generous liquid, and the man, more than half drunk, gladly filled his goblet to the brim.

Maxwell, though in no mood for revelry, was still less disposed for solitude. Half stunned by the blow he had received, he yet dreaded the moment at which he must stand face to face, as it were, with his great sorrow, and caught eagerly at any interval of delay as a respite from his sufferings. A draught of the rich, generous wine seemed to restore him somewhat to himself. Riccio, meanwhile, trolled off, in his mellow southern voice, a few notes of an Italian drinking-song.

He was no mean physiologist, the little Secretary, and he saw that his man was weary and saddened, and both morally and physically overpowered. So he gave the charm time to work, and when his companion had emptied the cup, poured him out another forthwith.

'Master Maxwell,' observed Riccio, as he marked the eye of the former brightening and the colour returning to his cheek, 'the ladies of the Court vow you are a true knight. Like our chevaliers of Italy, sworn before the Peacock to do them service, you are bound to refuse no adventure in their behalf. Is it not so?'

Maxwell winced a little. The subject was no pleasant one, and he was at this moment particularly sore on that point, so he answered in a cold hard voice,

'I have little respect for the mummeries of chivalry, Signior Riccio. A man should do his duty, whatever it be, for its own sake. And as for the ladies,' he added, with a sad smile, 'I leave it to younger and happier men to fulfil their wishes; if indeed they are fortunate enough to be able to find them out.'

The Secretary laughed gaily.

'Is it so?' he said, 'must all men alike discover that the little finger of a white hand is heavier than the arm of a Douglas sheathed in steel? I thought it was a lesson only learned by the dwarfed, the mis-shapen, the unsightly, like me. But you, master Maxwell, the handsome, the straight, and the tall; can it be that a woman listens unmoved to such men as you?'

There was no covert sarcasm, no leavening of ill-nature in his voice—nothing but the good-humoured banter of a laughing boon-companion. And yet it may be, that even under his jest, David Riccio was glad to learn that the prizes of life did not fall so readily to those personal advantages which he coveted with all the longing of deformity.

'Enough of this!' replied Maxwell, interrupting him rudely, and holding out his cup to be filled yet once more. 'Months of Holyrood have not succeeded in making me a courtier. I love the free open sky, better than these tapestried walls. I love the sound of a trumpet better than a woman's false whisper, and the shaft of a Jedwood-axe better than an ivory fan. I can hearken to a plain tale, and accept a defiance given in my teeth, but I have no skill in reading the thoughts of others by the rule of contrary, and I never could understand our Scottish proverb that averreth how "Nineteen nay-says make half a grant."'

He was still chafing under his ill-usage, and talking more to himself than his companion.

The latter looked at him long and eagerly. Apparently satisfied with his scrutiny he patted him on the shoulder once more.

'You are young,' he said, 'you have life before you; you are quick-witted, brave, and adventurous. What, man, there are more prizes than one in the lottery! If love be a false jade, ambition is a glorious mistress. Is it not better to sit at the back of the stage and pull the strings than to be one of the puppets and dance because another moves you. Perhaps a fool's dance, with a fool's guerdon for your pains at the end?'

Maxwell shook him off impatiently.

'You speak in riddles,' said he, 'and I have no skill

in expounding such parables. If you have aught to say, out with it, like a man. Midnight is already past.'

'And a fresh day begun, added Riccio, 'a fresh day, a fresh scheme, a fresh triumph. What say you, master Maxwell, have you stomach for an adventure? Have you a mind to draw your riding-boots on for those silken hose, and don corslet and head-piece on a Queen's errand? Or are *you* too under the spell that paralyses youth and strength and manhood? Are *you*, too, bound to some slender wrist by the jesses you dare not break, and a prisoner here at Holyrood because the rosy-lipped gaoler will not let you go?'

Maxwell laughed a fierce wild laugh, and dashed his goblet down upon the board with an emphasis most unusual to him. Though habitually possessed of much self-command, for an instant the tide of his feelings surged up beyond control.

'Holyrood!' he exclaimed mockingly, 'what is Holyrood to me? One place is like another, and all are barren! Talk not to me of jesses. Your wild-hawk soars her pitch, and strikes her quarry, and buries beak and singles in the dripping flesh, but, bird of the air though she be, she knows the false from the true, and will not stoop to the lure. There is no spell can fetter the limbs of a brave man who is determined to be free, and be the gaoler never so fair, I would not waste a look over my shoulder at my prison-house for the sake of the rosiest pair of lips that ever were kissed on the dawn of St. Valentine! Again, what is it you would with me, Signior Riccio? Were it an errand to the gates of hell, I think I have spurs that would serve me to ride there; and in good faith,' he added in a lower tone, 'a man need hardly wish to come back even thence to such a dreary world as this.'

Not a whisper of his voice, not a shade on his countenance, escaped his sharp little companion. What cared *he* how hot the furnace were, so that it tempered the tool aright. Nay, he was even willing to burn his own fingers a little, rather than fail in perfecting his instrument. At heart he thought how lucky it was that there should be men who allowed themselves to be influenced by less rational feelings than those of self-interest and ambition. Perhaps he felt something between pity and ridicule for that morbid state of mind, which could forget its own advantage, in anger, or pique, or sorrow. His swarthy face, however, wore nothing more than its usual expression of comical good-humour, as he linked his arm in Maxwell's, and fixing his twinkling eyes upon him, said,

'You are more trusted than half the peers in Scotland—aye, and more trustworthy too. Come with me to the Queen's chamber.'

Thus speaking, he led Walter out of the banqueting room and along the dim passages, in which the lamps were now expiring, to the foot of a winding stair, the same up which 'Dick-o'-the-Cleugh' had twisted his great body, under the guidance of Mary Seton. Here the Secretary paused for an instant and listened cautiously. It was pitch dark, and he gave his companion a hand to guide him through the obscurity, then opening a narrow door, and pushing aside a heavy curtain of tapestry, ushered him into a blaze of light and the presence of four ladies, crowded together in so small an apartment that Maxwell actually touched the robe of one of them while he entered, and was somewhat abashed to discover that its wearer was no other than the Queen.

It was Mary's custom, when the pageantry or duty of the day was over, to retire to this narrow retreat and sup in the strictest privacy, with two or three of her ladies at most. The proportions, indeed, of the apartment would admit of no larger party, as its area was little more than twelve feet by eight, and of this circumscribed space a wide chimney and a window occupied a large share. It was here that, at a later period, the shrieking Riccio clung to his Queen for the protection she strove to extend to him with all a woman's pity and more than a woman's courage; it was here that, in brutal disregard of her majesty, her beauty, and her situation, the high-born ruffians of the Scottish peerage butchered their victim before her eyes, nay, clinging to the skirts of her garment, and laid the weltering body down, within a few feet of her, to soak with its blood the very planks of their Sovereign's bed-chamber.

But to-night all was a blaze of light and warmth and comfort. The table, with its snowy cloth, was drawn close to the crackling wood-fire, which sparkled and glowed again in the cut crystals and rich plate that adorned the choice little repast; an odour of some rich incense, such as is burnt in Roman-Catholic churches, pervaded the apartment; and the strings of a lute that had just been laid aside were still vibrating from the touch of a fair and skilful hand.

The Queen herself, all the more lovely from the slight languor of fatigue, sat at the supper-table with her relative, the Countess of Argyle, a lady whose flaxen locks and ruddy laughing face formed no bad foil to the delicate colouring and deep, thoughtful beauty of her Mistress. Mary Seton, all coquetry, animation, and vivacity, as usual, busied herself in arranging and disarranging everything on the table; whilst another lady, turning away from the rest, with her head bent low over her task, was disposing some winter flowers in a vase with peculiar care and attention. It needed not the turn of her full white arm and dimpled elbow, nor the curl of rich brown hair that had escaped over her shoulder, to tell Walter this last was his *hated* love, Mary Carmichael.

The Queen gave him her hand to kiss as he entered the room.

'Welcome, master Maxwell,' said she, 'rather to the simple dame who has bid you visit her here, in private life, than to the Scottish Queen at Holyrood. We have put off our royalty with our robes. To-night we shall charge you with an errand that affects the woman far more than the Queen; to-night you must be less than ever our subject, more than ever our friend. You are faithful and trustworthy we know; and, indeed, there are few men on whose truth a lady would offer to stake her life,' she added, smiling, 'as one of mine did, not five minutes ago, on yours.'

Mary Seton laughed and pretended to hide her face in her hands.

Walter looked wistfully in the Queen's face; he did not turn his eyes towards Mary Carmichael, or see how the white neck had turned crimson while Her Majesty spoke.

'I can trust you, Maxwell?' added the latter after a pause, in her frankest and most engaging manner.

'To the death! Madam,' answered he in a tone of suppressed emotion; 'I have but little merit, I know, but I am as true as the steel I wear; I would give my life for your Grace willingly, now, this very minute!'

'I believe thee,' said the Queen, exchanging at the same time a rapid glance with Mary Seton; 'I trust, however, mine errand may be done without shedding of blood. Nevertheless, Maxwell, it requires courage, discretion, above all a silent tongue and a faithful heart. Listen! My good Sister entertaineth causeless grudges against me; she will endeavour to thwart my aim and cover the mark I shoot at; she liketh not of marrying nor giving in marriage. It may be that she mistrusteth her own power to rule in that state,' added Mary while a gleam of feminine vanity crossed her brow. 'It may be that Elizabeth hath more dominion over men's heads than their hearts; nevertheless, if she and her agents were to suspect thee of bearing such a secret of Mary Stuart's about thee, they would probe for it with their daggers but they would find it, ere thou wert a dozen leagues across the Border. Bethink thee, man, 'tis a dangerous burden; ar't not afraid to carry it?'

'Your Majesty is jesting with me,' replied Maxwell raising his head proudly, almost angrily, 'and I can but answer with a jest; yes, I fear to do your bidding as I fear a good horse when I am in haste, a cup of wine when I am thirsty, or a down pillow when I am weary and would fain lay my head down to rest.'

Mary Carmichael shot at him one glance of ineffable

pride and tenderness, then buried herself amongst the flowers deeper than before. He could not see it, his head was turned towards the Queen; he had not forgotten, no, he never would forget, the embrace of that stranger in the Abbey-garden.

'I knew it,' exclaimed Her Majesty triumphantly; 'believe me I was indeed only jesting with my brave and well-tried servant. Listen then, Walter! To-morrow you must be in the saddle at day-break; I reckon on your arriving at Hermitage before night-fall.'

At the name of Hermitage the Queen lowered her eyes for an instant, and looked somewhat confused ere she continued.

'In that stronghold you will find the Earl of Bothwell, who has returned with no leave of mine from his well-merited banishment in France; nevertheless, "a Queen's face should show grace," and we women forgive more readily than you of the sterner sex. You will summon him to appear before his Sovereign in Holyrood, so shall he receive pardon for his errors. Or stay, this were an ungracious behest to so tried a servant for one venial offence; you shall bear him Mary Stuart's full and free forgiveness, and bid him, as he loves his Queen, bid him on his loyalty and allegiance, that he speed with all his heart and all his strength the object of your journey.'

'And that object, Madam?' enquired Maxwell observing that Mary paused, blushing rosy red and averting her eyes from his face.

'Is my coming marriage,' proceeded the Queen hastily, whilst Lady Argyle and mistress Seton interchanged an arch glance and smile. 'An alliance that I take Heaven to witness, I contemplate more for the welfare of my people than for any foolish longings of my own weak heart. Henry Stuart is of royal blood, no unworthy mate for the proudest princess in Europe. Lord Darnley is a comely, gentle, and well-nurtured youth, of whose affection any lady in the land might well be proud. You will explain this to Bothwell; you will teach him that Mary has made no unworthy choice; you will tell him that she has confided in him, her old and tried servant, because she can depend upon him more securely than on any other lord in Scotland.'

'Would it not be well, Madam, to write the Earl a few lines with your own hand apprising him of your intentions?' hazarded Maxwell, who was sufficiently a man of the world to appreciate the delicacy of his mission; and who, in good truth, was sufficiently familiar with the temper of his powerful kinsman to relish not the least, the delivery of the message with which he was charged.

Mary, however, would not entertain such a proposition for a moment, and hurried on with far more of agitation than the occasion seemed to warrant.

'Letters may be intercepted, changed, forged, misunderstood. Master Maxwell, you will fulfil my bidding as I charge you, or leave it alone. I can trust you I feel. I know you will do justice to the fair intentions of your Mistress. I know you will not allow Bothwell to misunderstand my motives, or my feelings—Bothwell, who has always believed so implicitly in his Queen! Nay, for letters,' added Mary, with her own sweet smile softening and brightening her whole countenance, 'I will charge you, indeed, with this one for my Lady of Lennox, and with this token, always subject to his mother's approval, to be given as an earnest of my good-will to her son. Take them carefully, master Maxwell. Our Warden's strong hand will pass you safely through the thieves that infest the Border, and when you get among the Southrons, I know you will guard them with your life. I pledge you, my trusty messenger, to the success of your mission!'

While she spoke, the Queen filled out a cup of wine and put her lips to the brim, handing him, at the same time, a packet carefully sealed and secured with a silken thread, which wound in and out, through the folds of the missive, so that the silk must be cut before the letter could be opened. Also a small casket, containing a beautiful antique ring, representing a cupid burning himself with his own torch, as a keep-sake for her future husband. The messenger received them on his knees in token of his fidelity and obedience, and the Queen, according to the custom of the age, bade him finish the cup of wine in which she had recently pledged him, and refresh himself ere he departed.

'It must be a stirrup-cup, your Grace,' said Maxwell, with a smile; 'I shall hope to be out of sight of Holyrood ere the sun rises. Have I received all your Majesty's directions?' he added, preparing to take his leave.

'There is no such hurry for a few minutes,' replied Mary graciously. 'Do you sup with Royalty every night, master Maxwell, that you are in such haste to be gone?'

But Maxwell was enduring an amount of pain to

which he would willingly put a period. To be in the same room with Mary Carmichael, nay, so close that her very dress touched him when she moved, and yet to feel by her averted face, by his own offended and aching heart, that they were completely and irrevocably estranged, was a trial to which he had no wish to subject himself for a longer time than he could help.

'I must crave your Grace's license to depart,' said he; and added, looking round with a forlorn hope that just this once he might meet the eyes that he had resolved should never gladden him again, 'Have none of your ladies any commands for merrie England or the Border?'

Mistress Carmichael stirred uneasily, and grew very pale, but she neither looked at the speaker nor answered him. Mary Seton, however, with rather a noisier laugh than common, charged him with a message on her own part, of which, as she said merrily, he was not to purloin nor spill any portion by the way.

'If you should chance to see that rude giant who calls himself Lord Bothwell's henchman,' said that young lady—'tell him from me, that I hope he has not forgotten, in his wild glens, all the polish we had such difficulty in imparting to him at Holyrood. Commend me to him, in sober earnest,' added she demurely; 'I would send him my love had I not the fear of mistress Beton before my eyes, for in good truth he is the only honest man I know in Scotland, except yourself, master Maxwell, and you are so stern and unforgiving, that I am quite afraid of you. If a woman loved you ever so dearly, I think you would give her up or the slightest misunderstanding.'

The shaft might have been shot at random, but it pierced home to at least two hearts in that little supper-room. For an instant, *his* eyes met *hers*, and that sad, reproachful imploring glance, haunted him afterwards for months. Then Mary Carmichael, pale, proud, and sorrowful, turned away from him once more to her former occupation, and Walter Maxwell, taking a respectful leave of the Queen, was ushered by Riccio from the presence.

As he sped southward through the chill air of morning, after the few hasty preparations had been completed for his departure, he could not but acknowledge that the world had never seemed so dreary, that he had never felt so sick at heart before. Perhaps it would have cheered him though, to know that another's sufferings were even keener than his own, lying broad awake behind him there at Holyrood, pressing a pale cheek against a pillow wet with tears.

CHAPTER XXIX.

> 'But had I kenned or I cam' frae hame,
> How thou unkind wad'st been to me,
> I would have kept my Border-side,
> In spite of all thy peers and thee.'

'HOOD her up, Dick! The worthless haggard! Like all her sex, I would not trust her a bow-shot out of hearing of the whistle, out of sight of the lure. Curse her! I should have known she was but a kestrel. By the bones of Earl Patrick she shall never strike quarry in Liddesdale again!'

The Warden was in a towering passion. His favourite hawk, a bird that he had chosen to name 'The Queen,' had not only missed the wild-fowl at which he had flown her, but spreading her broad pinions to the wind, had sailed recklessly away for several miles ere he could recover her, a salvage that had only been made at considerable expenditure of patience and horseflesh.

He was now standing by the side of his panting steed at the head of one of those deep, grassy glens which give such a pastoral character to the wilds of the Scottish Border. A severe and exhausting gallop the Warden must have had to judge by the condition of the bonny bay, whose heaving sides were reeking and lathered with sweat; yet the good horse pawed, snorted, shook himself, and got back his wind, ere the rider recovered his temper.

'Dick-o'-the-Cleugh,' too, had mercifully taken his long body out of the saddle, and was now busy replacing hood and jesses on the recent captive.

'There's no siccan a falcon 'twixt here and Carlisle,' said Dick, smoothing with no ungentle hand the neck-plumage of the refractory wild-bird. 'Whiles she'll gang her ain gate when she misses her stoop, and what for no? a falcon's but a birdie when a's said and done, and she's just the Queen of Falcons; bonny and wilful as a queen behoves to be!'

Bothwell turned angrily upon his follower. The Warden's temper had become more violent and uncertain than ever.

'Hood her up, man, I tell thee!' said he with an oath or two, 'and fasten up my girths; it is time we were back at Hermitage.'

Thus speaking he threw himself into the saddle, and followed by his henchman, proceeded down the glen at a gallop.

The Earl was at this period of his reckless and chequered life, perhaps more than at any other, a dissatisfied and miserable man. After his imprisonment in Edinburgh Castle subsequent to his brawl with the Hamiltons, an imprisonment he felt he did not deserve, at least at the hands of the Queen, he had returned to his fastness in Liddesdale, where he had been obliged to remain in a state of seclusion and inaction, extremely galling to one of his adventurous nature and ardent temperament. Here he received no direct communication from Mary herself, a neglect which irritated, whilst it distressed him, and he only heard of her continued displeasure through others in whom he could place no reliance, and whose interest he more than half suspected it was to create dissension and mistrust between him and his Sovereign. He then went for a short period into France, hoping perhaps that this self-imposed exile might elicit a recall to Holyrood; but finding no notice taken of his movements, and assured on all sides of the Queen's continued coldness, he returned to his strong Castle of Hermitage in a maddening state of uncertainty as to the future position he should assume. The wild borderers were all as devoted as ever to their chief. He had at no time been actually deprived of his office as Warden of the Marches and Lieutenant of the Southern Border, nor, had he been superseded, was it probable that a successor could be found bold enough to take upon him the duties of the office. Accordingly the Earl remained at Hermitage in the anomalous position of a Sovereign's representative whilst held to be an avowed rebel to that Sovereign's authority; in the agitating dilemma of one who is at variance with the person to whom he is most devoted on earth, and whom Self-love forbids to offer that reparation which Pride whispers may be contemptuously refused.

The Warden galloped on in silence for several minutes, till the nature of the ground and the jaded condition of his good horse brought him perforce to a more sedate pace. With an impatient jerk at the bridle and a curse on the stumble that provoked it, he relapsed into a walk, and summoning 'Dick-o'-the-Cleugh' to his side, proceeded to vent the remainder of his petulance on his companion. That worthy's good-humour, however, was proof against all such attacks, and Bothwell, calming down after a time, took back the favourite falcon to his own wrist, and began to caress the bird whose wild flight had so much aroused his wrath.

'"Tis a royal pastime, in good truth, Dick,' said he as they emerged from a deep narrow glen, and beheld, spread out before them a broad expanse of moorland, patched and brown and sombre, yet suggestive of sport and freedom, a sound sward whereon to breathe a horse, and a soft grey winter's sky in which to watch the flight of a hawk. 'I would rather be here in the saddle than mewed up in the old keep over yonder,' pointing while he spoke to the square towers of Hermitage, looming dim and grand in the distance; 'would rather handle any weapon than a pen, and track any slot rather than unravel a cipher. I marvel that the Earl of Moray can keep his chamber, as he doth, the livelong day, writing, plotting, calculating; never a stoup of wine to cheer his heart; never a breath of the free air of heaven to cool his brow. I'll wager you a hundred merks, Dick, that how long soever he remains in my poor castle he never sets foot beyond the moat till the stirrup-cup is in his hand.'

'The brock* likes fine to lie at earth,' answered Dick, with a loud laugh, 'and I doubt there's no a brock in Liddesdale that's a match for the Earl of

---

* The badger.

Moray in takin' his ain part. But hegh! Warden, there's a sight for sair een!' exclaimed the henchman, interrupting himself suddenly. 'See to yon canny lad ridin' down the glen; if yon's no maister Maxwell may I never lift cattle nor plenishing more! I wad ken the back o' him 'mang a thousand. 'Odd, man! but ye're welcome to Liddesdale again.'

In truth, while the borderer spoke, Maxwell made his appearance on the track that led to Hermitage, exchanging, as soon as he spied the Earl and his henchman, for a brisk hand-gallop the more steady pace at which he had been prosecuting his journey. The greeting between the kinsmen was sufficiently cordial, between 'Dick-o'-the-Cleugh' and the new arrival, of the most boisterous and demonstrative nature. The rough borderer would have been at a loss to explain to himself why he entertained so warm a regard for Walter Maxwell. As the three rode slowly on together towards Hermitage, the emissary thought it a good time to broach the business which had been intrusted to him by his Sovereign.

Slowly pacing over the open moor, where everything breathed peace and repose, where not a tuft of heather stirred in the soft still air, and the call of a moor-fowl or the dull flap of a heron's wing alone broke the surrounding silence; where the softened gleams of a winter sun came down in sheets of mellowed light, and heaven above and earth below seemed wrapped in security and content, Maxwell poured into no inattentive ears the tale that was rousing all the fiercest passions of our nature in the heart of one of his listeners.

Bothwell, after bidding him a hearty welcome to the

Border, heard him patiently and in silence, with an enforced composure that was more ominous of subsequent evil than would have been the wildest outbreak of that wrath which he suppressed with such an effort. His jaded horse, indeed, felt his rider's thighs tightening on him like a vice as the tale proceeded, and exerted himself gallantly to meet the unusual pressure; but only a very close observer could have marked, by the clenched jaw, the widened nostril, and dilated eye, that every word was driving its sting deeper and deeper, poisoned and festering, into the Warden's heart.

Once indeed when a brighter gleam of sunshine than ordinary lighted up the moor, and the old towers of Hermitage coming into view imparted a picturesque and even beautiful aspect to the scene, Bothwell looked up to Heaven as if in helpless expostulation with the mocking sky, and then in one bitter and defiant smile, took leave for ever of those nobler and better feelings which had hitherto redeemed his character from utter reprobation.

It was at this moment that Maxwell urged his kinsman to forward him at once upon his journey.

'I will but break bread with you, my lord,' said he, 'and so with a fresh horse speed my way to the southward once more; mine errand brooks no delay, and he that goes wooing for a Queen must not let the grass grow under his feet while he is about it.'

'Is her Grace indeed so hurried?' answered Bothwell with an evil sneer. 'Can she not wait a matter of twenty-four hours, more or less, for this long, smooth-faced lad on whom she has set her princely heart so wilfully? God speed the royal wedding say I,

and good luck to the bold suitor who would lie in a
Queen's bed! Here, Dick, your horse is fresher than
mine, gallop on to the Castle and bid them prepare
for master Maxwell's refection; see, too, that the Lord
Rothes' men and horses be well looked to if they be come.
I have guests to-night with me at Hermitage, Walter;
I pray you be not so niggardly as to depart without
a supper and a night's rest. It is ill travelling on the
Border after night-fall, and I will speed you on by sun-
rise to-morrow with the best horse in my stable and a
guard of my own men. And now that long knave is
out of ear-shot, tell me, master Maxwell, is this marriage
but an affair of state and policy? or doth the Queen
seem to affect it for herself? Is her heart in it think
you?'

While he asked the question Bothwell busied himself
about the hawk on his wrist, it may be to conceal the
trembling of his lip, which extended itself even to his
hands, for his strong fingers seemed unable to take
off her hood or loose the fastenings that secured her
jesses.

'In faith,' answered Maxwell honestly, 'her Grace
bade me make no secrets with your lordship. When
she spoke of marriage her colour went and came like a
village maid's going a-maying; I reck but little of
such follies,' he added with a sigh, ' but if you ask me
the truth, I think, Queen though she be, she loves him
as a woman should love the man whom she bids to
share a throne.'

Bothwell swore such a fearful blasphemy that his
companion, whose attention had been somewhat engrossed by the irregularities of the track, looked up

astonished in his face. The Earl excused himself by vowing that his falcon had struck her talons into his arm.

'The foul-hearted haggard!' he exclaimed, flinging the bird violently from him into the air, 'let her fly down the wind to the Solway an' she will! She may stoop on the southern side ere I whistle for her; no such false kestrel shall ever perch on wrist of mine again.'

The hawk soared freely up into the soft calm sky, then spreading her wings to the breeze, sailed gallantly away to the westward, and was soon out of sight.

Maxwell was too good a sportsman not to be surprised at such an action on the part of his host, but attributed it to one of those outbreaks of temper in which he had heard the Earl was prone to indulge, and as they now proceeded to the Castle at a gallop by the Warden's desire, who spurred his tired horse with savage energy, he had no opportunity of pursuing the subject on which they had been engaged.

That evening, however, there was much consternation amongst the retainers on discovering that 'the Queen' was missing from her mews; much discussion as to who should take upon himself the perilous task of informing the Chief of his loss; much astonishment at Bothwell's unexpected answer to the stammering varlet who apprised him of it,

'May the foul fiend fly away with every feather of her! Never speak of her again! Go fetch me a stoup of wine.'

In the meantime the Earl and his guest sprang from their reeking horses at a postern-door which admitted them privately into the Castle of Hermitage. Already its court-yard was filled with the retinue of the Lord Rothes, a powerful Fifeshire baron, who had even now arrived with no inconsiderable following, on a visit to the disgraced Warden. His men were well-armed and determined-looking, their horses strong, swift, and of considerable value. It argued little for the repose of the country, when lord met lord upon a peaceful visit, with fifty or a hundred spears at his back.

Extorting an unwilling promise from Maxwell that he would partake of his hospitality for one night, a concession only made by the latter on the express agreement that relays of horses should be sent forward immediately to enable him to prosecute his journey with extraordinary speed on the morrow, Bothwell placed his guest in the hands of an elderly person, whose black velvet dress, white wand, and grave manners, could only belong to the *major-domo*.

'See my cousin well-bestowed in the eastern turret,' said the Warden, 'and bid them serve supper without delay. Tell Lord Rothes I will give him a welcome to my poor house the instant I have doffed my soiled riding-gear. Bring me the key of the wicket in the winding-stair, and tell 'Dick-o'-the-Cleugh' to have six picked men and horses ready to-morrow at day-break.'

With many grave deliberate bows the old man received the orders of his Chief, and then preceded Maxwell solemnly to his chamber, while Bothwell with swift irregular strides, betook himself up a winding staircase to a chamber in a remote tower of the Castle.

Knocking, but not waiting for permission to enter the apartment, he walked hastily to a table at which a man sat writing, who looked up on his approach. Then, with an expression of irritation and impatience at the calm face that met his own, Bothwell flung himself into a chair, and commenced pulling and twisting the long moustaches that overhung his mouth.

Moray, for it was the Queen's illegitimate brother, whose occupation the Warden had interrupted, looked at his host with his usual wary scrutinizing expression that seemed to extract the thoughts of others, but afforded no clue to his own. It was a handsome face too, this mask so well adapted to conceal the workings of a mind in which diplomacy stifled every instinct of manhood, every chivalrous spark of honour, loyalty, and good faith. The bright fair complexion, the regular features, the keen grey eyes, deep-set, and glittering with scornful humour, forcibly repressed, the thin closed lips, shutting in, as it were, upon an ill-omened smile, and the broad square chin, denoted rather the daring schemer than the dashing soldier, the wary politician to whom, so as it led at last to his object, the path was none the less welcome for being devious, rather than the stout-hearted champion who would break his own way for himself through every obstacle, with his own right hand.

Gravely and plainly dressed, though in a rich suit of sad-coloured velvet, adorned with costly pearls, the figure that supported this inscrutable face was formed in fair and graceful proportions. The manners of the man were those of an accomplished courtier dashed with something of that stealthy gravity which marks the Romish priest; yet Moray was now of the strictest amongst the Reformers.

'A shining light,' so said the followers of John

Knox, 'an advanced disciple and assured professor of the true faith!'

'Mine host appears disturbed,' said Moray, in the low impressive tone which acted as a sedative on all who came within its influence. 'What ails ye, my Lord Earl? Hath your falcon flown so high a pitch she will perch on your wrist no more? or have our friends on the southern side so far forgotten themselves as to drive a raid across the Border? I think we have influence with the English Queen for "heading and hanging" at Carlisle as promptly as at Jedburgh!'

Bothwell winced. Hating the intrigues in which he found himself involved; balancing, as it were, on the verge of a precipice to which his passions hurried him, and from which his better nature held him back, he loathed in his heart the master-spirit that he was yet fain to obey. The demon was under the spell of the magician, but his submission was as unwilling as it was complete. He burst out angrily,

'See to what your schemes and your intrigues have led at last! Is this the upshot of my Lord of Moray's plotting and counter-plotting, and Randolph's promises, and Maitland's crabbed ciphers? Faith! a couple of hundred spears and a closed horse-litter would have done the work long ago far better than all your bonds and all your treaties. And now it is too late. The noblest Queen in Europe, the fairest woman on earth, is to be wasted on a half-witted boy, a beardless minion of the English Court. Out upon you, Earl Moray! I have worn steel since I was twelve years old, and man hath never so deceived me yet. Again I cry shame on you! Answer me how you will!'

If Moray was startled at the intelligence or angered at the manner in which it was conveyed, neither sensation was suffered to betray itself for an instant. He smiled pleasantly on his chafing companion, and answered composedly,

'All's not lost that's in hazard. Surely no lord in Scotland knows this better than the Warden of the Marches. Tell me the worst intelligence you have gained, and how you learned it.'

Moray's brow grew darker and darker as his host detailed to him, not without violent gestures and many a wrathful expletive, all he had gathered from Maxwell concerning the Queen's proposed marriage. Whether new to him or not, the intelligence seemed to give him great concern, and once, although it was now twilight, he turned his face from the window so as to conceal its expression from his dupe. When Bothwell had finished his story there was a dead silence for a few minutes. He had lashed himself into a violent passion; he was now calming down into a sullen despair. Moray's face, on the contrary, wore a brighter look after he had ruminated awhile, but his voice was as cold and distinct as ever when he spoke again.

'And the messenger is here, you say; here, in this very Castle. Lord Bothwell, if we gain time, we can place the pieces on the chess-board for ourselves. Your borders here are not without their disadvantages. 'Tis bad travelling for single horsemen; they may be robbed of letters and even jewels. Nay, if they make much resistance they are sometimes heard of no more. 'Tis a numerous family, the Maxwells, and a loyal. One more or less makes no such great odds.'

'Nay, nay, he is my kinsman, urged Bothwell,' who perfectly understood the dark suggestion of his guest, but to whose frank and ardent nature such counsels were most distasteful. 'Besides, she trusted me; she trusted me. My Queen's own words were, that "she could depend upon me more securely than on any lord in Scotland."'

'You best know the value of the stake you play for,' answered Moray, with a very sinister smile, 'and the amount you are willing to set against it. Master Maxwell is a trusty messenger, no doubt, and will do his part faithfully, an' he get not his throat cut ere he reach Carlisle. Should this marriage ever take place it will be prudent, Lord Bothwell, for you to make early court to young Henry Stuart. He has a noble future before him in truth. The Crown-matrimonial of one kingdom, the Crown in reversion of another; a Catholic alliance, or I am much deceived, with France, Spain, and Austria; lastly, no small temptation, Lord Earl, to young blood, Her Grace, my sister, the fairest woman in Europe, for a bedfellow. In good faith the prize is worth struggling for!'

The arm of the chair which Bothwell held broke short off in his hand.

'Enough!' he exclaimed, 'it shall never be. What! am I not Warden here? Have I not power of life and death on the Marches? But no blood shall be shed; no blood, Moray. Can we not bestow him in safe keeping? Counsel me, my lord, for I am at my wits' end.

Moray laughed outright.

'I will tell you a story,' said he, whilst he shuffled

his papers together and tied them up, preparatory to changing his dress for supper. 'When we were studying at college in France, my brothers and I had great dread that the prize would be carried off by one of our companions who had more book-learning than all the rest of us put together; well, we invited the clever youth to an entertainment, and we drenched his brains with wine—just such a red generous Bourdeaux as I saw a runlet of pierced only yester even here in the buttery—then we tied him on a horse, a sorry French nag enough, but able to carry him some ten leagues away into the country, where we left him to sleep off his carouse. When he returned next day the examinations were over, and I myself, for as dull as you may think me, had taken the first prize. All is fair in love and war, my lord. The curfew is already ringing, it is time for both of us to meet Rothes at the supper-table.'

The hint was not thrown away upon Bothwell.

'I will bestow him securely,' said he, as a bright idea seemed to flash across him, and he too departed hastily to make preparations for meeting his guests at supper.

Contrary to the usual custom of Hermitage, this meal, instead of being served in the great hall and shared with Bothwell's jack-men and retainers, was brought into a smaller apartment furnished with extreme splendour, and as near an approach to luxury as the times and locality permitted. This was perhaps done as a compliment to the presence of Moray, who was already beginning to accustom the nobility to his assumptions, and while he treated them with the outward cordiality of an equal, to cozen them insensibly of the attentions due to a superior.

The dishes were served with great pomp by the grave *major-domo* and two staid attendants splendidly dressed; the Lord Rothes, a dark handsome man with a sinister expression of countenance, sat on the left hand of his host, Maxwell faced the latter, and the Queen's half-brother was in the place of honour on his right; also Moray's chair was somewhat higher than those of his companions, and of a different form.

When the meal was over, the wine according to custom, circulated freely; whatever designs might be lurking in the breasts of the four men, the conversation was merry and jovial enough, embracing the usual topics of hawk and hound and horseflesh, with a good-humoured gibe or two at the opposite sex and a free criticism of their charms.

Maxwell might be pondering on the difficulties of his task; Moray weaving additional meshes in that web which entangled himself at last; Rothes reflecting on his frailties or his debts, his past follies or his coming embarrassments; and Bothwell eating his own heart in combined pique, disappointment, and vexation; but each man filled his cup, and pushed round the flask, and passed his frank opinion or his loud jest, with a merry voice, an open brow, and a cordial smile upon his face.

When the wine began to take effect, Maxwell excused himself from further participation in the carouse, and asked permission to retire on the plea of his early departure in the morning. After a faint resistance exacted by the laws of hospitality, Bothwell acceded freely to his request; meditating as he did, a foul treachery against him, the Earl felt his cousin's absence would be a relief. Moray, indeed, would have had small hesitation in so spicing his wine that he would need a sleeping-draught no more, and few scruples would have deterred Rothes from ridding himself of a troublesome guest with six inches of cold steel; but the Lord Warden had still some rough soldierlike notions of fair-play about him, had not lost all at once every trace of the chivalry and manhood that had made him heretofore the stoutest champion of his Queen.

When Maxwell had retired, his host sat moodily for a while, wrapped in meditation, drinking cup after cup in gloomy silence, and playing ominously with the haft of his dudgeon-dagger, a weapon that was never for an instant laid aside.

Moray seemed to divine his thoughts. After a few whispered words to Rothes, who treated the whole affair as an excellent jest, he observed in a cold measured voice, and as if continuing the thread of a conversation in which they had already been engaged,

'You cannot so prudently bestow him here, my lord, though it were a good jest to keep a Queen's ambassador mewed up in a Queen's fortress, and the prisoner would be well lodged with his affectionate kinsman.'

'Why not?' demanded Bothwell, rather fiercely. 'The walls of Hermitage are pretty strong, my lord, and these riders of mine are held to have a somewhat close grip when once they lay hold.'

'Nevertheless,' argued the other, 'this would be the first place suspected. Nay, it might be well that you should even deliver up the Castle to Her Majesty with a clean breast. I have thought more than once of urging you to demand an audience at Holyrood, to resign your lieutenantcy or obtain a just acknowledgment of your loyalty from my royal sister.'

Bothwell's face brightened.

'True!' he exclaimed, dashing his heavy hand on the board. 'We must have no stolen horse in the stall when the ransom is told down! A clean breast and a "toom-byre,"* as we say here on the Border. I must send him elsewhere.'

Rothes filled his cup, with a laugh.

'I can lodge him at Leslie,' said he; 'any kinsman of Lord Bothwell's is welcome in my poor house. "Food and wine he shall not lack," as the old song says; aye, and a bed, too, my lord, if so you will it, that shall serve him till doomsday.'

Bothwell flushed dark red with wrath and shame.

'Not a hair of his head must be jeopardied!' he exclaimed passionately, then controlling himself, added in a more friendly tone, 'I am beholden to you, Leslie, nor will I forget your courtesy. I shall, indeed, commit my kinsman to your care for a brief space. Four of my knaves, commanded by one whom I can trust, shall convoy him to-morrow into Fifeshire; though its Lord is here with so gallant a following, Leslie House is, doubtless, not left ungarrisoned.'

'Trust me for that!' answered Rothes, an evil sneer again marring the beauty of his countenance. 'They are peaceful knaves enough, the men of Fife, yet they would like well to harry the old corbie's nest

---

* An empty cow-house.

up yonder, and clear off scores for a few of Norman's doings, to say nothing of my own. It will be long, though, ere they crack the stones of my poor fortalice with their teeth, and I care not to ride in Fife without some fifty spears at my back; there are more than as many there even now. Hark ye, Bothwell, take my signet-ring here; give it to your lieutenant, and he will find himself at Leslie House " master and more." '

Moray, pretending not to listen, now asked for more wine with a great assumption of joviality and recklessness. A close observer, though, might have remarked that he scarce touched his own cup with his lips, whilst he encouraged his companions, who indeed were nothing loth, to empty theirs again and again. Artfully leading the conversation to the Queen's possible marriage, to her different suitors, and other topics connected with Mary, he watched Bothwell writhing under the torture, and drowning his sufferings in revelry, with covert interest tinged by a sardonic amusement.

It was midnight ere the reckless orgy broke up, when Moray, calm, cool, and smiling, bade his companions a placid ' good-night ;' while Rothes, flushed and boisterous, trolled off a ribald drinking-song; and Bothwell, in whom wine had been powerless to drown the stings of conscience, sought his solitary chamber, with keen remorse and torturing self-reproach gnawing at his heart.

CHAPTER XXX.

'In solitude the sparks are struck that bid the world admire,
Though heart and brain must scorch the while in self-consuming fire.
In solitude the sufferer smiles, defiant of his doom,
And Madness sits aloof and waits, and gibbers in the gloom.
'Tis dazzling work to weave a web from Fancy's brightest dyes,
And speed the task ungrudging all we have and hope and prize.
But it must make the devils laugh, to mark how day by day
The plague-spot widens out and spreads and eats it all away.
In vain the unwilling rebel writhes, so loth defeat to own,
And strives to pray, and turns away, and lays him down alone.
Oh! better far to moan aloud, on earth and heaven to cry,
Than like the panther in its lair, to grind his teeth and die.
Then help me, brother! Help me! for thy heart is made like mine;
The shaft that drains my life away is haply winged for thine.
It is not good to stand alone, to scorn the rest, and dare;
But two or three, like one must be, and God shall hear their prayer.'

HEATED with wine, stung with jealousy, torn by conflicting feelings, Earl Bothwell paced the stone floor of his bed-chamber, as a wild beast traverses to and fro between the sides of its cage. His step had the same noiseless elasticity, his air the same subdued ferocity, his eye the same lurid sparkle that seems struck from some quenchless fire within. If there are

indeed hours at which the master-fiend is permitted to vex those human souls, who, for some wise purpose, are delivered like Job into his hand, the Lord Warden must have been that night a prey to the arch-enemy of our race. It needed but little addition to the frenzy of his mood to imagine a dusky shape, defining itself more and more distinctly in the gloom, stepping as he stepped, turning as he turned, whispering in his ear suggestions that curdled his very blood while he pondered them, and yet were tinged with the strange fascination which all frantic expedients possess for despair. It takes a long apprenticeship to sorrow ere a man can bow his head in resignation and cease to struggle, nay, even to quiver under the lash ; but he who has gained this faculty at the cost of anguished moments, none but himself and one besides can count, is indeed master of his fate.

Such, however, was far from the condition of the tameless border-lord. He could have fought, struggled, died with the fiercest champion that ever set his teeth in the grim smile of a death-grapple ; but the Hepburn blood was not the stuff of which martyrs are made, and the fiercest scion of all the bold, bad men that constituted the pride of its line, was now, so to speak, like some demoniac of antiquity, wrestling and striving against himself, torn and rent and infuriated by the possessing spirit, which refused to be exorcised and come out of him. That night in his lonely room at Hermitage, Bothwell learnt many new and strange things, never to be forgotten whilst he had life. Depths of guilt, into which heretofore he would not have dared to look, were now opened up to him, and there was seduction in the very immensity of the abyss. Crimes, dazzling from their boldness, now seemed feasible, nay, almost justifiable, and entranced him by the reckless daring with which they must be carried out. He had been dreaming hitherto a soft sweet dream for years. He was awake now, broad awake, and the vision should become reality, or he would never dream again. He had been cozened long enough! 'What? the game was not yet played out. Turn and turn about, fair dame! and it was Bothwell's turn now!' He laughed a low hissing laugh within his beard, and then stopped, startling in his walk, for it seemed to him that the laugh was echoed by something in the room, and that the shape was close to his ear now, whispering, whispering, one continuous stream of upbraiding and persuasion and reproach, with maddening promise and stinging sarcasm, and here and there a devilish scoff.

But these paroxysms wear themselves out. By degrees the Earl became calmer; by degrees he recalled the past and reviewed the present, and looked steadily on the future. The whirl of contending passions passed away to make room for a stern and gloomy resolve far more dangerous, and the molten stream of thought that had seared his brain, cooled down into the settled determination of the man.

There are seasons when the whole of our past lives seems presented to us as on a stage, each scene distinct and vivid as when it actually took place. Men are taught to believe that this occurs at the supreme moment ere the spirit leaves its dwelling, and when the heart clings so instinctively and so pitifully to its treasure *here*. Be this how it may, there can be no doubt that at periods of strong excitement, this *clairvoyance*, if we may so call it, acquires extraordinary power. For a moment it seemed to Bothwell that the gloomy walls of his chamber had disappeared, and he stood again beneath the sunny skies of France. Again the towers of Joinville started from the smiling plain, and he knelt once more to tender his homage to the fair widowed bride, who looked so sweetly down upon him, with her pleading womanly beauty, softening and enhancing the majesty of a Queen. It was the first time he had ever looked on that face, which, despite of all his madness, all his crimes, was imprinted thenceforth on his rebellious heart. He had seen it since in sorrow, in triumph, in levity, nay, in bitter anger and unjust displeasure against himself, but it was still the same face to him, the type of all that was pure and good and lovely upon earth, the charm that had wound itself into his whole being, that shed its magic glow over every scene and action of his life; whether he laid spear in rest, or flung his hawk aloft in air, or watched the last rays of sunset gilding the broad brown moor on a peaceful summer's evening, still that face was ever present to him, with its quiet, thoughtful beauty, and the kind look in its deep winning eyes; then he thought of the many, many times when he had vowed in his heart to cherish undying love and loyalty for her alone, to ask no happier fate than to suffer shame and sorrow for his Queen. Would he not have given his life-blood for her, oh! so gladly that morning at Holyrood, when he alone of all her nobles had grieved with her on her day of grief, when, overcome by his faithful sympathy, and stung by the cold ingratitude of the rest, she had turned her face away and wept? And was he so changed now that he could be plotting treason against his Sovereign and violence towards his love? For a moment his better nature mastered him; the fierce set features writhed, the strong frame shook, and though he was alone in the room, in the hush of midnight, the proud noble bowed his head and turned his face aside, ere he dashed away the drops that had stolen unawares to his shaggy eye-lashes.

But the Devil was watching his opportunity, and what a picture did he now conjure up! The beautiful Queen in her robes of ceremony, with the crown upon her head and the orb and sceptre in her hands; ambassadors from England, France, Spain, Austria, thronging with their sovereigns' congratulations; the nobility of Scotland proffering homage before the throne; and these regal honours shared by a tall handsome stripling, who would lift his lady-face scornfully, and stretch a weak girlish hand for *him*, Bothwell, to kiss! Worse than all, amongst the courtiers' jeering faces, Moray's cool sardonic smile, as of one who had foreseen the degradation from which, had his advice been taken, it would have been so easy to escape. And then the banquet and the wedded pair, sitting side by side, and the subsequent revel, and the customary ceremonies, and the laughing guests departing one by one,—and then, and then,—the stillness of night brooding over the old pile of Holyrood, and Mary once more a bride, another's bride, and Bothwell a laughing-stock! * * *

'Perdition! it shall never be!' exclaimed the Earl, dashing down, while he spoke, with the violence of his involuntary gesture, the lamp that stood on the table by his side. The few moments consumed in rekindling it gave him time to compose himself, and to determine on his future conduct. It was but a brief period, yet was it long enough for Bothwell to bid farewell, at once and for ever, to all the higher and purer feelings of his nature; to change him from a man who with many faults and with ungovernable passions, yet possessed a certain frank uprightness, a certain chivalrous devotion to the one idol of his life, into an unscrupulous ruffian, prepared to commit any crimes, to go any lengths in the prosecution of his schemes, and willing in brutal selfishness to drag his idol down to the dust, rather than see it enshrined upon the pedestal of another. One moment cannot indeed change the whole character of a human being, though it may influence his whole conduct; but as it is the last ounce that breaks the patient camel's back, so is it the one additional atom of sorrow, or unkindness, or disappointment, added to the mass, that overwhelms the poor sufferer's powers of endurance, and drives him into the frenzy of despair, or leaves him stunned and sick at heart, in the helpless apathy of a ruined man. It would be well to think of this sometimes when we see the bruised reed so nearly broken, the kind generous nature so wearied and suffering and overladen. It is but an ignoble triumph to lend the tottering mass that slight push which sends it crashing to destruction. It is cowardly and un-English to 'strike a man when he is down.'

Bothwell lit his lamp, and, wrapping a furred bedgown around him whilst he thrust his feet into the *mules* or slippers which would best muffle their tread, proceeded with swift and stealthy strides along the

passages of his Castle, towards the eastern turret in
which his kinsman was disposed. All was hushed and
silent within the walls of Hermitage. The drowsy
sentinels might have been sleeping on their posts, for
neither stir of arms nor measured tread of steel-shod
foot denoted their vigilance, yet, strange to say, the
Warden failed to observe this unusual silence. Nevertheless, pre-occupied as he was, he marked a light
still burning in Moray's chamber, and instinctively he
shaded the lamp he carried with his hand when he
passed the narrow casements on the opposite side of the
Castle-yard. Arrived at Maxwell's door, he listened
for a while and satisfied himself by the deep breathing
within that his kinsman was asleep; then shading his
light once more, he entered the room softly, and made
at once for the small travelling valise, in which he
hoped to find the messenger had secured his despatches.
But Maxwell had travelled the Borders ere this, and
had profited by his experience. Ready dressed, booted
and spurred, with his sword by his side, he lay prepared for a start, sleeping indeed, yet not so sound but
that a sudden noise might waken him. Whatever he
had about him of value was concealed in his breast, and
could not be taken from him without disturbing his repose. Bothwell felt once for the haft of his dagger,
and smiled grimly to himself, as he thought how easily
he might possess himself of his guest's despatches, and
how lightly he would think *now* of such a crime as
murder under his own roof. There was even a wild
devilish triumph in the reflection that he could have so
changed within an hour!

After a moment's thought, however, he again passed

unobserved from the room, and returned to his own as stealthily as he had come. There he spent the remainder of the night, still pacing up and down, up and down, and an hour before dawn summoned 'Dick-o'-the-Cleugh,' already astir thus early, to a long and mysterious consultation, in which, though he yielded eventually, for the first time in his life the retainer presumed to remonstrate with his lord.

CHAPTER XXXI.

'Oh, they rade on, and farther on,
  And they waded through rivers above the knee,
And they saw neither the sun nor the moon,
  But they heard the roaring of the sea.'

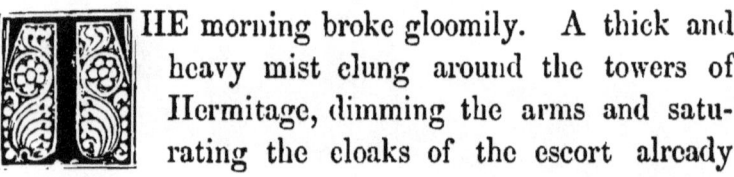

THE morning broke gloomily. A thick and heavy mist clung around the towers of Hermitage, dimming the arms and saturating the cloaks of the escort already mounted and waiting in the Castle-yard. The moisture dripped from the ears and nostrils of the horses, and stood upon the beards of their riders, while the former stamped and shook their bits impatiently, and the latter muttered a coarse jest or two, not without fervent aspirations after a tass of brandy to keep the raw air from their throats.

Presently, 'Dick-o'-the-Cleugh' emerged from the turret containing the Warden's private apartments, wearing an unusually gloomy expression on his face, and proceeded to examine the arms and appointments of his comrades, with a disposition to find fault that elicited sundry growls, murmurs, and a round oath or two, from the impatient jack-men.

There was, however, but little delay in starting the

cavalcade. Maxwell, who had been anxiously awaiting the spare horse prepared for him, was soon in the saddle exchanging a cheerful greeting with the troopers, to which Dick alone made no reply; and while it was yet scarcely light, the portcullis was raised, and the party filed out, intently watched from one of the narrow windows by a haggard eager face, that still looked and lingered after the croup of the last horseman had disappeared. Bothwell even made one hasty gesture as if to re-call his mandate, and order the party back, but changing his mind again on the instant, with a bitter laugh, he took a long draught from a wine-flagon that stood by his bed-side, and then flinging himself on the couch, turned doggedly to the wall and tried to force his senses into sleep.

Maxwell felt his Sovereign's letter lying safe within his doublet. He examined too, the priming of his pistols, and turned his sword-belt a little more to the front. Then he proved the mouth and mettle of his charger, with rein and spur, deriving from the experiment, all the confidence felt by a good horseman on a well-bitted steed. Satisfied at length on these important points, his spirits rose with the morning air and the excitement of his mission. Even Mary Carmichael's falsehood seemed less black in hue than it appeared yesterday. The future once more showed promise of something beside a dull apathetic response to the call of duty alone. He looked along its dim vistas, and saw the light shining, though faintly, at a distance. The mission was already in imagination half-fulfilled. He had made his journey prosperously through the rich districts of middle England, and gained the capital with unprecedented rapidity, thanks to good luck in procuring horses, and his own untiring powers in the saddle. He had delivered his credentials to Lady Lennox and presented himself at Greenwich Palace to the Maiden Queen. He could even conjure up a picture in his mind of that redoubtable lady. Could imagine the flaxen curls, the stately figure, the harsh yet not uncomely features, and the dignified gestures that veiled a woman's vanity, beneath the majestic bearing of a British Sovereign. He became a courtier for the occasion, and thought how he could serve his own dear Mistress with a well-timed compliment, and a little apt flattery to her rival ' Good Sister.' He saw himself dismissed with honour, and speeding back to the North triumphant at the safe accomplishment of his mission. Then he fell to thinking of Mary's kindly thanks delivered with all that charm of manner, which made a word from her better than a jewel from another, and his welcome reception at Holyrood by all the loyal and well-disposed party to whom it was of no small moment to see their Queen happily married.

Perhaps *others*, thought Maxwell, might not have served her so well. Perhaps *one* of her maidens with whom, as with the rest, loyalty was still the master-passion, might be inclined to give him a welcome far warmer and kinder than her proud and distant farewell: might think she had judged him harshly, prematurely; might wish when it was too late that she had not so scornfully rejected his devotion, nay, might long to possess now what she had valued so lightly when it was her own. Then he would teach her a lesson that it would do her good to learn; then how delicious would be the triumph of meeting her coldly, politely, with calm friendship and quiet good-will, far more cutting than any amount of assumed indifference and unconcern; then she would know that she had altered her mind too late, that a man of energy and action was not to be pulled hither and thither like a puppet by the weak hand of a woman holding the string; that she had flung the falcon from her wrist once, jesses and all, and he would soar his swing now, and never stoop to lure of hers again.

Oh! it would be a happy moment; and yet how much happier to forgive her freely, and without reproach to take her hand in his, look frankly in her face, and tell her he had loved her all along, even when she was most wilful and most unkind! Was he not a man—a bold strong man? What had he to do with pride as regarded her? Nay, was it not his pride to think that whilst he yielded an inch to no one else on earth he would always be content to accept suffering, sorrow, even humiliation for her dear sake?

Such is the usual conclusion of one of those love reveries in which men indulge whilst under the influence of the malady; such is the climax of an infinity of stern resolution and haughty self-reproach and bitter self-examination; we make ourselves very unkind and very uncomfortable, and after all leave off very much at the point from which we started, if anything, in a less rational frame of mind than at first.

Maxwell could not but compare himself at the moment to the horse of one of the leading files of his escort, which had got bogged up to the girths in a *well-*

head, as those particularly soft pieces of morass are called, which abound on the Scottish moorland. The poor animal made two or three gallant efforts to extricate itself, stimulated not only by the great terror a horse entertains of such a catastrophe, but by a fierce application of its long-legged rider's spurs; each plunge only hampered it more irrevocably, and at last amidst the loud jeers of his comrades and a volley of oaths from himself, the trooper abandoned the saddle and wisely allowed the beast to be still for a few moments and recover its wind.

Maxwell's attention which had hitherto been somewhat taken up with his own thoughts was now directed towards the locality in which he found himself, and the mist clearing away as the day drew on, enabled him to recognise one or two of those acclivities and breaks of the sky-line which constitute the land-marks of an open moorland district, such as he was at present traversing.

Though he had been but once before at Hermitage, his soldier's eye had not failed to acquaint itself with the general outline of the surrounding country. He now recognised a conical-shaped hill on his left hand that he distinctly remembered to have passed yesterday in riding from Edinburgh on his right; the wind too, which from the appearance of the weather he judged to be easterly, struck cold upon his right cheek; he was convinced they must be going North. His first impression was that the party had lost its way in the mist; his first impulse to jeer its leader, his old friend, Dick, on such a want of moss-trooping sagacity.

'How now, master Dick?' said Maxwell, cheerily,

looking round for his friend, who rode silent and sullen in the rear, 'I should have thought you knew your way to the southern side better than this! If you wanted to drive Lord Scrope's horses, or empty a byre or two in Cumberland, you wouldn't take the road to Holyrood, as I am much mistaken if we are not doing, this morning. Why, man, I came by that very cairn on the green hill yesterday. Thou must be asleep, Dick, for I know the ale is not yet brewed that will make thee drunk!'

Dick shook himself sulkily in reply, and moving his horse alongside his questioner, laid his hand on the other's bridle-rein as if to guide him into a sounder path.

'I'm thinkin', maister Maxwell,' said Dick, with an assumption of extreme friendliness and great caution, 'that it wud be mair wise-like just to whig cannily back to Holyrood, and leave a fule to gang a fule's errand for himsel.'

Maxwell laughed good-humouredly. Even now he was persuaded the borderer had missed the southern track, and was annoyed at his own stupidity, perhaps inclined to veil it from his men by affecting ignorance of his charge's destination.

'Holyrood is a fair palace, Dick,' said he, 'and I left it but yesterday at day-break. Do you think I came all the way to Hermitage only to push the wine-cup round with wild Lord Rothes, and so back again with red eyes and a singing brain, to my duties in the Queen's ante-room? Nay, nay, the sooner we strike the right track and cross the Border the better. Why, man, I should be half-way to York before sun-down!'

Dick seemed sadly disturbed. He fidgeted with his bridle, he loosened his sword in its sheath, he looked up and down and on all sides of him in obvious vexation. Once when a jack-man rode nearer Maxwell than was convenient, he bade the man keep his distance with a hearty curse. He seemed hurried, and yet anxious to put off time, and talked at random as one does who has some engrossing subject of no pleasant nature to occupy his thoughts.

'Ye wad be better at Holyrood, maister Maxwell,' said he, still harping on the old subject, 'An' ye were at the Palace yesterday, nae doot, wi' the Queen an' her leddies, an' who but you? I wish ye were there at this moment, maister Maxwell, an' that's the dooms truth o' it!'

'Orders must be obeyed, Dick,' answered the other, vainly trying to induce the whole cavalcade to increase their pace which had now dwindled down to a very funereal walk. 'That reminds me, I have a message for you from one of the Queen's maids-of-honour.'

All the blood in the borderer's great body seemed to rush into as much of his face as was visible beneath his morion, then the colour faded visibly, and for the first time in his life 'Dick-o'-the-Cleugh' turned as white as a sheet.

'It wad no be from mistress Seton!' said he, almost unconsciously, and with the true Scottish negative that affirms so much. 'Man! I wad like fine to hear it,' and he bent over his horse's neck and looked Walter in the face with something of the wistful eager expression that the Newfoundland dog, to whom he has already been compared, assumes when his master is going to throw a stick for him to retrieve out of the water. In the animal goes! A plumper off the pier, be it never so high, and the waves breaking never so angrily below, and you may be sure that in his noble instinct of fidelity he would drown ten times over before he would let go.

Walter freed his rein from the other's grasp, and struck into a trot.

'It was but to hope you had not forgotten all she taught you, Dick, good-manners and such-like. I may tell her when I see her again that you are such a courteous squire now, you guide the bridle-rein of a mounted man-at-arms as carefully as a lady's palfrey. Tush, man! we are wasting time, let us strike into the right path and get on. I tell thee mine errand admits of no delay!'

He spoke impatiently, but yet in perfect good-humour, and looking on his companion's face, was startled at the expression of intense pain that was apparent in its features. 'Dick-o'-the-Cleugh' looked like a man who had been shot through the body, and was endeavouring to hide his internal agony under an appearance of outward composure.

Inside that stalwart frame of his a terrible conflict was going on. Good feeling, manhood, a certain reflective sense of the duties of hospitality, above all, loyalty to the Queen, represented by an intense devotion to one of her maids-of-honour; all these sentiments were at war with the habits of a life-time and the first feudal instinct of the henchman—implicit obedience to his Chief. It is needless to say that the latter obtained the mastery.

Maxwell was a friend, and he had come from the immediate presence of her who was the one bright image that gladdened the man's honest unsophisticated heart, that elevated his rude nature and gave him a glimpse of something better than clash of steel and clang of drinking cups, the excitement of a foray and the pleasures of a debauch: but, on the other hand, Bothwell was the master whom he had venerated and obeyed from childhood; whose mandate it never occurred to him to dispute; whose will was law. The Rutherfords had served the Hepburns by flood and field as long as either family could count their line. It was not for Dick, so he thought, to be the first traitor of his race; yet he loathed his task, too, this frank-hearted borderer, and his face was very stern and his voice rung hoarse and harsh when he spoke again.

'Ye say true, maister Maxwell. Orders *must* be obeyed, Gude forgie' us! and *the Laird's bidding must be done!*'

Startled by the altered tone Maxwell turned in his saddle, and at the same instant a thick woollen plaid, thrown over him from behind, was drawn tight across his head and face, a sword-belt was as quickly strapped round his arms above the elbows, a stout moss-trooper pinioned him on either side, two more were at his horse's head, his weapons were secured, and he found himself, in the space of about half-a-minute, helpless, blindfold, half-stifled, and a prisoner!

Accustomed as he had been in his adventurous life to every sort of catastrophe, the present seemed to him the most unaccountable and startling of all. He had not witnessed the chafing Warden's interview yesterday with calm, impassable, unscrupulous Moray, nor guessed how much he had to thank his host that imprisonment rather than death was his present fate. He knew nothing of the conclave held over their wine after he had retired last night by the three nobles, when Rothes had suggested so jovially that he might be blinded or left in a dungeon for life, or hidden out of the way altogether, in any manner that was most agreeable to his boon companions.

'For,' as the peer politely put it, while he filled his cup to the brim, 'you need have no fear of inconveniencing *me*. We have a saying in Fife of which I have always endeavoured to uphold the truth—"Ask no questions of the Leslies, for their answers are sharp, silent, and to the point." If he goes down a certain winding-stair in my poor house you might never hear of him again till you wanted him; and, if need be, I could produce you his bones, at any rate, twenty years hence. Do not hesitate, I pray you, I am only happy to accommodate the Warden. Bothwell, your good health!'

Nor had he overheard the orders accepted so unwillingly by poor 'Dick-o'-the-Cleugh' an hour or two before dawn, nor that worthy's eager remonstrance and extreme unwillingness to fulfil his Chief's behests. Perhaps the henchman never felt so keenly that he was a vassal as when he told off six stout jack-men for the unwelcome duty, and informed them of the catch-word, '*the Laird's bidding*,' at which they were to muffle and pinion their prisoner.

Maxwell knew it was useless to complain. A request for a little air was so far complied with that the plaid, while it still blinded him, was enough loosened to admit of his breathing more freely; but no answer was vouchsafed to the few indignant questions that, in his first surprise, he had put to his captors. The pace, too, at which they were now going, forbade conversation, and, in the few words exchanged at intervals between the jack-men, their prisoner failed to distinguish the tones of 'Dick-o'-the-Cleugh.' Notwithstanding the henchman's treachery, Maxwell's heart sank a little within him to think that he was deserted by his last friend.

After many hours of hard riding, and when he could not but feel that his horse was becoming completely exhausted, the fresh sea-breeze made him aware that he was approaching the Firth. With no unnecessary violence, though with much rapidity, he was, ere long, lifted from the saddle and placed in a boat, but the plaid was still kept round his head, and an unbroken silence preserved even by the men who handled the oars. It must have been long after night-fall when they made the opposite shore, and Maxwell, despite his hardy frame, was becoming faint and exhausted from fatigue, vexation, and want of food.

As he was again forced into the saddle, however, a flask of brandy was applied to his mouth, and at the same time a strong bony hand grasped his own warmly, and 'Dick-o'-the-Cleugh's' welcome voice whispered in his ear,

'Tak' anither sup, lad, and keep your heart up. Ye've gotten a friend to your back for a' that's come and gone yet.'

CHAPTER XXXII.

'Good morrow, 'tis St. Valentine's day
All in the morning betimes,
And I a maid at your window
To be your Valentine.'

HERE is one Saint in the Calendar, who at least has never lacked worshippers. At whose shrine the strictest sectarians, the bitterest Reformers, have never failed to lay their votive offerings, and in whose train shine myriads of the brightest and fairest beings we can picture to ourselves, the only Angels that gladden the sight of us adoring mortals here below. Yes, blooming maidens, buxom widows, constituting a phalanx beautiful to look upon, as it is dangerous to deal with, have for centuries conspired to do honour to sweet St. Valentine, and we can only regret, that the anniversary of his martyrdom (kissed to death, we have always been taught to believe, and buried by turtle-doves under a shower of orange-blossoms) should occur at a season of the year when in our own climate the usual concomitants of frost and snow seem so inappropriate to the indolent and relaxing amusement of love-making. We have no reason to believe that the 14th of February, 1654, afforded any contrast to the usual boisterous inclemency

of a Scottish spring, or that Queen Mary and her
maidens looking from the battlements of Wemyss Castle
on the leaden waves of the stormy Firth, had any sunshine to gladden them save that which originated in
their own breasts.

But the Queen at least was in the height of good-humour and good spirits; though subject to occasional
fits of depression, Mary's usual state of mind was
kindly and cheerful; nay, when in some rare interval
of peace she was relieved from the pressure of actual
distress, or the anticipation of impending calamity,
her gay and cordial manner shed an influence of happiness over all who came within its range, and even
Randolph,—busy, intriguing, heartless, cynical Randolph,—could not but admit that 'this Queen,' as he
calls her, ' is a divine thing, far excelling any (our own
most worthy only excepted) that ever was made since
the first framing of mankind.'

Behold then, Mary Stuart and her maidens sitting
at work in a chamber overlooking the stormy Firth
from the sea-ward turret of Wemyss Castle. Without,
the leaden hues of sea and sky form a grand though
savage contrast to the white snow-mantle which wraps
the undulating shores of Fife, while the opposite
Lothian coast stands out, as it were, into the water
with the distinct outline and startling appearance of
proximity peculiar to an atmosphere charged with
coming snow, and a wind from the north-east.

Within, an old oak-panelled chamber, hung here and
there with faded tapestry, once of priceless value, but
now frayed and worn and coming rapidly into rags;
grotesque, gaunt ornaments are strewed about the room,

the spoils of predatory warfare on the Danish coast, brought hither generations back by stern Sir Michael, the first Lord Admiral of Scotland. Strange looking arms and a ponderous axe or two are not in character with the interior of a lady's bower, nor do the grim figures carved in wood that support the chimney on either side of the high wide fire-place, the least resemble such cupids and other gentle symbols as would be appropriate to the company and the occasion.

Bending over her work, the Queen's blushes come and go with a degree of graceful embarrassment that is not unmarked by her attendants. These are around her as usual, and, like their mistress, occupy their fingers with considerable energy, and doubtless allow their thoughts to stray far and wide during the task. We of the sterner sex have probably not the faintest idea of the comfort derived by woman from her natural weapon, the needle.

It is well known, we are told, to physiologists, and the fact is not lost sight of in our treatment of the insane, that manual labour requiring a moderate amount of attention, such as the prosecution of a handicraft, has a remarkably composing tendency on the mind; but carpentering is perhaps the only male pursuit which combines the exact proportions of physical and mental exertion supposed to produce such beneficial results. Few men, however, are carpenters, whereas, speaking in general terms, all women can sew, and the very act of stitching we believe to be a complete and unfailing anodyne. The delicate fingers bend unconsciously to their task, the white hand flies to and fro as the dove flew round the Ark seeking the olive-branch on which it should find rest at last: the gentle head bends lower and lower, while thoughts, humbled by sorrow and chastened by resignation, wander farther and farther away. Presently the tears are dropping fast upon the pattern, be it the beads of a queen's embroidery or the hem of a peasant's smock; but like summer showers they do but clear the sky when they are over, and ere the hair is shook back, and the loving face looks up to thread the needle afresh, all is sunshine and peace once more.

Perhaps no woman of any degree had oftener occasion to practise this healing occupation than ill-fated Mary Stuart, destined to a pre-eminence in suffering as in beauty.

The only male attendant on the Queen was David Riccio. Splendidly dressed in the thickest velvet that could be procured, that poor little Italian shivered in a corner of the ample fire-place, preserving, to his credit be it said, his southern good-humour even in the rigours of a cold, raw climate, which, to use an expression from his own land, seemed 'to loosen every tooth in his head.'

Three of the maids-of-honour were unusually silent and depressed, Mary Seton alone incorrigible as usual.

A portentous shiver from Riccio, which he tried in vain to repress, made the Queen look up from her embroidery. She could not but smile at the chattering teeth and pinched features of her ungainly Secretary, yet there was a slight tone of irritation in her voice as she said,

'Heap more wood on the fire if you are so cold, Signior David; yet methinks the weather hath moderated since morning. It cannot be so bad even now on the landward side; but the wind whistles round this old keep of my brother's till we might fancy ourselves a plump of wild-fowl cowering together for shelter on the Bass.'

Her eye happening to rest on mistress Beton while she spoke, that demure lady, who was plunged in a profound fit of abstraction, felt herself called upon to reply, and could find nothing more apposite to say than,

'Bitter weather indeed, your Grace, and threatening worse than ever over the Firth. Heaven help all poor travellers by land and sea!' she added, piously, drawing at the same time her mantle closer round her shoulders to the utter destruction of her stupendous ruff, a neglect of which ornamental structure always denoted in Mary Beton extreme discomposure of mind.

'Psha! child!' said the Queen impatiently, 'Travellers are not so faint-hearted. What say you, Signior David? We wot of some that would ride through fire and water at our behest. Is not that the gallop of a horse I hear even now along the causeway?'

'I pray you patience, Madam!' answered the cautious Italian, seeing that the Queen had risen from her chair and was pacing up and down in obvious expectation. 'No traveller that your Grace wotteth of can be on this side the Firth to-day. Spurs are but steel; horses are but bone and sinew; riders but flesh and blood. There can be no arrival at the earliest for twenty hours. I have myself wagered a collar of pearls and rubies with mistress Seton.'

'And lost! and lost! and lost!' exclaimed that

voluble young lady, dancing rather than walking into the room from which she had not been five minutes absent. 'Even now the portcullis is up, and I saw him myself ride into the court-yard from the passage window. Good lack, Madam, such a tall cavalier! and his poor horse looked so tired! Not a living creature with him neither, and he called for a cup of wine before ever his spurs had touched the pavement.'

Mary Stuart's cheek turned very red, and her breath came quick and short; the Woman could not but appreciate the compliment, however much the Queen must study to conceal her feelings. This looked like an earnest wooer in good truth; no laggard could thus have distanced his followers and arrived in such an incredibly short space of time from the southern shore. Aye! there was more lost and won on that ride of young Lord Darnley's than the collar of pearls and rubies which David Riccio delivered the same evening with such a good grace to saucy mistress Seton. But the Queen's innate dignity soon re-asserted itself. Signing to her ladies to attend on her, she paced majestically from the room.

'It would ill become us,' said she, 'to keep one waiting for an audience who hath shown such loyal diligence in obeying our summons; we will receive our guest in the great hall of the Castle. Do you, Signior Riccio, apprise him that we are ready to accept his homage. Mary Carmichael and Mary Hamilton attend us for a few minutes to our tiring-room; we will all meet again here, and proceed at once to the hall.'

Mary seldom spoke in such a measured dignified

tone. It may be that this stately manner covered some little trepidation and heart-beating; it may be that the Queen felt timid and bashful as the meekest village maiden. At least it was remarkable that the most beautiful woman in Europe should have thought it necessary to revise her toilet, and add to her attractions before receiving the homage of her vassal and kinsman.

It was no ordinary phalanx of beauty that Darnley had to confront when the venerable seneschal of Wemyss Castle ushered him into the lofty hall, at the end of which, on a portion raised by one step above the level of the floor, was placed the royal lady to whom he had dared to aspire as his bride; her exquisite loveliness only enhanced by the presence of the four prettiest women in Scotland who stood behind her. But 'faint heart never won fair lady,' and Darnley's was by no means one of those dispositions which are prone to fail from a retiring modesty and too low an estimate of their own advantages. Besides, he was playing a great stake, and playing it with all the reckless audacity of a gambler.

Young as he was, he well knew that the prize now before him represented not only the Majesty of Scotland, but possibly, nay, in all human probability, the eventual succession to the English throne. It was this contingency which made Elizabeth so jealous of all matrimonial overtures to her beautiful Cousin; it was this which caused Cecil and Throckmorton and their agent Randolph to lay their cunning heads together and devise means for amusing the Scottish Queen with a procession of suitors, none of whom were ever intended to be more than the puppets of the moment, each to prevent the attainment of his object by the other.

The accomplished Warwick, the manly-looking, weak-hearted Norfolk, nay, the prime favourite of the English Queen herself, the selfish, handsome, and utterly unscrupulous Leicester, were successively put forward as appropriate sharers of Mary Stuart's throne and masters of her hand. But no sooner did the hapless object of all this intrigue and duplicity show the slightest preference for one over the other, the faintest inclination to accede to wishes which seemed so candidly expressed, than instantly, like some scene in a masquerade, the performers all changed characters at once. Elizabeth became the stern monitress, Randolph the delicate adviser, and the belted Earls and noble Dukes, no longer humble suitors and devoted champions of their idol, cooled at a breath into very coy and somewhat unwilling parties to an engagement of political expediency, only binding so long as it received encouragement at Greenwich or Whitehall. Thus was a woman's heart made an object of cruel traffic and shameful double-dealing, none the less disgraceful because its possession implied the occupancy of a throne. Some day, perhaps, the world may be brought to see that even in the highest places expediency can never justify heartlessness or crime, that not only is 'honesty the best policy,' but that chivalrous unselfishness, and frank defiance of evil, are the surest beacons to success.

In the meantime, it is sad to think, that the life's happiness and the life itself of Mary Stuart were pitilessly sacrificed by one of her own blood and her own sex. Surely, since the Serpent, woman has had no such bitter enemy as woman.

Darnley, put forward at eighteen as the rival of so many distinguished nobles, entered on the contest with all the wilfulness of a Stuart, and all the joyous temerity of a boy. Though a tool in the hands of his seniors, it must doubtless have seemed to the adventurous young nobleman, no unwelcome task to woo his beautiful Sovereign—the kinswoman whom he had already once seen when they were both mere children, but whose charms even at that early age he had not yet forgotten. Few men would refuse the hand of a Queen, even if she were an ugly one; what shall we say of a proposal to try his fortune with such a paragon as Mary Stuart? It was no wonder the lightsome young wooer rode horse after horse to death as he posted northward in the direction to which his star beckoned him; no wonder that he should arrive at Wemyss Castle all alone, far ahead of his scattered escort; no wonder that he should advance into Mary's presence, under all the disadvantages of haste, fatigue, and travel-stained riding-gear, with the gallant air of a gay young knight who goes forth to conquer, rather than of a slave who comes to wear a chain. As he walked up the hall, his step was firm, his head erect, and his eye bright and open as that of a man who sees his destiny beckoning him forward fairer and fairer, more and more promising as he approaches.

The colour was very deep in Mary's cheek, and her eyes were fastened to the ground while he drew near, yet she stole a good look at him somehow, too, or she would not have been a woman. What she saw might have satisfied even her fastidious taste.

Darnley was very tall and slim, but his limbs were so well-proportioned, his hands and feet so small and beautifully shaped, that his excessive height only gave him an air of peculiar grace and distinction above ordinary men. Even in the riding-dress of the period, though we may be sure that the handsome young noble wore one of the richest material and of the most tasteful fashion such a costume allowed, he betrayed those habits of refinement, almost bordering on coxcombry, which, when they accompany a fine manly person, have such an attraction for the other sex. All the details of his toilet had been carefully attended to before he started, and disordered as he now was, at least on his exterior, nature had written *gentleman* in characters that could not be mistaken. Alas! that her pen can sometimes only trace skin-deep.

His face too was in accordance with the high-bred beauty of his form. The line of features was soft and delicate as a woman's, the dark eyes shone out soft and tender from beneath a pair of pencilled eye-brows, the dark hair clustered in silken curls round a fair and open brow, pure and unruffled in the calm spring-time of youth, and though the mouth was that of a voluptuary rather than a hero, the small teeth were so white and regular, the lips so full and red, that, had it not been for the down beginning to shade its contour, it might have belonged to a girl. The whole countenance would indeed have been too effeminate, but for a bold sparkle in the eye, which corresponded well with the manly proportions of the frame.

The subject was not half so much abashed as the Sovereign. Darnley advanced confidently up the hall, then kneeling before the Queen and kissing the hand she tendered him, he looked boldly in her face and asked leave to deliver certain packets with which he was charged from his mother and kinsfolk.

'But your mails have not yet arrived, my lord,' said Mary. 'You have out-ridden your retainers; you are the only one of your party who hath yet reached us here in our hiding-place beyond the Firth.

She stopped in some embarrassment, unwilling that Darnley should learn how much his coming had been looked for and his arrival watched.

'I have them with me here, your Grace,' answered he, producing at the same time a packet from his bosom. 'I would trust my Queen's letters to no hands but my own, although to remind me of her I do not need to carry them next my heart.'

He dropped his voice at the latter part of his sentence, but looked her boldly in the face while he spoke, as if to mark the effect of his words. Boy as he was he knew well how to woo a woman already, and had not been slow to learn that the reticence of true affection is the worst auxiliary in the world. He had studied his own motto to some advantage this adventurous young suitor, and now or never was the time to say,

'Avant Darnlé,
D'arrière jamais.'

So he kissed the fair hand once more that took the packet from his own, and added,

'None of my servants can be here for hours, Madam, and I have dared to appear before your Majesty all disordered and travel-stained. May my rudeness stand excused in the ardour of my desire to see the beauty which now dazzles me so that I can hardly look upon it, and my loyal anxiety to obey the commands of my Mistress and my Queen? Am I forgiven, Madam? 'Tis said that " a lady's face should show grace."'

'And well it might, to such a face as yours,' *thought* the Queen; but she only answered a few words of common-place courtesy, bidding her cousin rise from his knees, and affected to busy herself in the packet of letters she had just received, for Mary was again blushing deeply, and not unwilling to hide her confusion in the task she had thus set herself. Truth to tell, though she had hitherto been so impervious to flattery, the words she had just heard were stealing their way very softly and pleasantly to her heart.

Seeing her thus occupied, Darnley proceeded to pay his compliments with graceful ease to the attendant ladies, finding time to note in his own mind, their respective attractions, and to discover that Mary Seton was the most to his taste of all the four.

After a while, and, it may be, somewhat disturbed in her studies by the merry voice of her gay suitor, who came (such is the advantage of being young) as fresh from his ride of so many hundred miles, as if he were lately out of bed, the Queen looked up, and with kindly courtesy bade him join them at the noon-day meal, then about to be served. The young courtier had the good taste to excuse himself, pleading the want of proper attire in which to meet Her Majesty at table, and reflecting in his own mind that he could satisfy the hunger which he now began to feel so keenly more comfortably alone. He saw too that he had made an agreeable impression, and wisely determined to give it time to work. So he asked permission to wait on his Sovereign at supper instead, and retired to refresh himself in private, and curse the delay of his servants whom he expected, hour by hour, with some portion of his baggage.

It may easily be imagined, that in the seclusion of Wemyss Castle, such an event as the arrival of a guest like Darnley created no small amount of excitement and conversation. Doubtless every point in his doublet, every hair of his head, was thoroughly discussed and criticized, in kitchen, buttery, and hall. The rumour spread like wild-fire through the Castle that this dashing springald was a suitor for the hand of the bonny Queen.

'Set him up!' as the Scottish lower orders say when they opine that the aspirant is hardly worthy of the prize. Nevertheless the young lord's height, appearance, and easy manners had already won him golden opinions of those who judge chiefly by the eye, and when he had finished the best part of a capon, and a goodly stoup of Bourdeaux for his breakfast, the old seneschal delivered himself of the opinion that 'the youth was a bonny lad, an' a fair-spoken—forbye bein' a Stuart himsel, an' no that far off frae him that lies out bye yonder at Flodden!'

Had there been any dissentients, an allusion to their favourite hero, James IV., would at once have brought them over to an agreement with the majority.

But in Mary Stuart's bower the engrossing theme

was canvassed with considerably less freedom. The Queen herself was restless and ill at ease, constrained in manner and reserved in conversation. Mary Carmichael was absent on certain household duties; Mary Hamilton seldom opened her pale lips now, save at matins or vespers, when she poured from them such floods of melody as if she were indeed an angel from that heaven to which she was so obviously hastening; mistress Beton had been too long a courtier ever to broach a fresh topic of conversation, or indeed to give an opinion frankly upon any subject whatsoever,—moreover she had no means of learning what Randolph said to all this, and she felt somewhat at a loss to form her own ideas without the assistance of her false English lover; Mary Seton alone led the charge bravely by asking the Queen point-blank what she thought of her young kinsman.

'Nay,' replied Her Majesty, with a smile, 'you would not have me give an opinion after a five minutes' interview. The *outside* methinks is of fair promise; at least if " all be good that be upcome." ' *

'Aye, he's well enough to look at,' answered the young lady, with the air of a consummate judge. 'Long and small, even and straight; a proper partner for a galliard, and, I should say, would grace velvet doublet and silken hose better than steel corslet and plumed head-piece. But *my* choice, now, would be something sterner, stronger, rougher altogether; something more of a *man*; like stout Earl Bothwell for instance!'

---

* A Scotch saying, equivalent to the converse of our ' Ill weeds grow apace.'

The Queen started as if she had been stung, and answered angrily,

'How mean ye? The one is a loyal and accomplished gentleman, the other a brawling swordsman and a traitorous rebel.'

'A woman might have worse help at her need than the Lord Warden in jack and morion, with a score of those daring borderers at his back,' retorted the staunch little partisan, following out, it may be, some wandering fancy of her own.

The Queen did not seem loth to pursue the subject.

'You were talking of looks,' said she, ' not swordstrokes, and Bothwell, at his best, was bronzed and marred and weather-beaten, and built more like a tower than a man.'

'That was exactly what I admired in him,' interposed the damsel; 'I even thought that scar over his eye became his face as it would have become none other.'

The Queen smiled once more and resumed, in the tone of one who is looking far back into the past,

'He certainly had more of the warrior than the courtier in him, and doubtless he hath always done his part well and knightly in the field; I will do him that justice. Poor Bothwell! he must have been ill-advised indeed when he could refuse to obey *me*. I thought I could have trusted him if all Scotland besides had failed me. Well—well, all must be forgiven now—and forgotten.'

She spoke the last words in a melancholy tone, and each relapsed into silence, for both the Queen and her damsel seemed to have ample food for thought; so their fingers flew over the tapestry more nimbly than ever, and the work proceeded with extraordinary perseverance till supper-time.

But if Darnley had been pleasant to look at in his travel-stained riding-gear, the most fastidious eye must have admitted that he was, indeed, splendidly handsome when he appeared, prepared to perform the menial offices of the Queen's supper-table, clad in a suit of gorgeous apparel, cut in the newest fashion of the English Court. Refreshed with food and repose, sleek from the bath and perfumes of his toilet, radiant with hope and excitement, the young courtier stood before his Sovereign probably the best dressed and the best looking man that day in her dominions.

After he had gone through the form of presenting Mary with the bason and ewer, which she declined, she bade him sit down at the same table with herself and her ladies, for the Queen disliked ceremony and always dispensed with it in private to the utmost. Then did Lord Darnley strain every nerve to be agreeable, and with so partial an audience, it is needless to say, succeeded beyond his highest expectations. Skilled in those outward graces which make so good a show and are so effective in society, it was an easy task to him, even in the presence of royalty, to lead the conversation round to those topics on which he was best qualified to shine.

His descriptions of his journey, his humorous account of the difficulties he experienced in procuring horses at the different posts, with a covert allusion here and there to his impatience to get on, were listened to with laughter and interest by all—with rising colour and heaving breast by *one;* while in no circle probably of either kingdom could his graphic sketch of the English Court, with its petty intrigues and latest scandal, have been appreciated with such thorough zest and goodwill.

It does not follow that Mary Stuart was displeased because she checked him when he mimicked her 'good Sister' to the life, hitting with a happy mixture of fun and malice, on some of the most prominent foibles and grotesque points in the character of 'good Queen Bess.'

Ere the ladies rose from table they had made up their minds that this new acquisition to their society was of unspeakable merit; and later in the evening, when they discovered that he could play and sing as well as he could talk, and that his leg and foot were as beautiful as his face and hand, Mary Seton had almost decided that such courtly graces as these were worth all the ruder virtues of a less accomplished gallant, and judging from her subsequent conduct, we may fairly conclude that Mary Stuart's opinion followed on the same side.

A few more days of the seclusion of Wemyss Castle, lightened by the lively talk and winning manners of the guest, served but to establish Darnley more securely in the good graces of his Sovereign. The weather was of unexampled severity, and a deep snow prevented all attempts at out-door amusements, and especially forbade those field-sports in which Mary took such delight. The society of a handsome young gallant, fluent and accomplished, was not likely to be rated below its real value, when it represented the only amusement available to five such ladies as the Queen and her Maries shut up in an old house during a snow-storm; and Darnley found he had free access at all hours of the day to their agreeable presence; but he had as yet enjoyed no opportunity of seeing Her Majesty alone. Mary, with her own good sense and womanly reserve, had resolved to judge for herself more at leisure ere she committed her happiness to the keeping of her possible husband, or encouraged him avowedly in his suit.

The young lord, however, impatient by disposition, and now reckless on principle, had resolved that this brief visit to the old sea-side tower should determine his fate; he would never have such a chance again; and on the last day of Mary's sojourn at Wemyss Castle he made up his mind to hazard all upon the cast.

Darnley entertained few scruples of delicacy when he had an object in view. He chose the hour when Mary Hamilton was sure to be in an oratory which the Queen had temporarily fitted up, to get the three other ladies out of his way: a few gold pieces judiciously administered induced the venerable dame who charged herself with the domestic details of the Castle, to request the presence of mistresses Beton and Carmichael on a visit of inspection to vast hords of linen hid away in an old walnut-wood press; then seducing Mary Seton into the long gallery under pretence of a match at billiards, or *bilies* as it was called, he coolly left the game unfinished and turned the key upon that young lady, who found herself, somewhat to her dismay, a prisoner in a remote apartment of the Castle without the slightest prospect of escape. Chance, too, further favoured his designs, for a blink of sunshine had tempted the Queen out upon the battlements, and he found her there alone, looking wistfully across the Firth towards the southern shore.

We are no eaves-droppers on the courtships of royalty. Turn after turn Mary Stuart paced up and down those leads, and still Darnley urged and argued and gesticulated, and still his fair companion blushed and listened and shook her head. That the interview was not entirely without results, Mary Seton gathered from what she witnessed at its conclusion. She had been released from durance by a domestic who happened to be passing the door of the gallery, and hastened immediately to excuse her absence to her Mistress; as she approached the battlements Darnley was offering the Queen a ring, with every appearance of eagerness and agitation, and although the latter obviously declined the gift, it was with a kindliness and an embarrassment that made the refusal tantamount to an acceptance.

'For *my* sake,' said Darnley imploringly, 'your subject, your vassal, your slave for ever!'

'Not yet,' murmured the Queen in answer, and although she spoke very low, her whisper reached the keen ears of the attentive maid-of-honour.

As Darnley left the presence he did not stop to apologize to Mary Seton for their unfinished match. His colour was high, his eye was very bright; there was an air of joyous triumph in his whole aspect and bearing: perhaps he was quite satisfied in his own mind that he had won the game.

CHAPTER XXXIII.

'We'll hear nae mair lilting at the ewe-milking,
Women and lasses are heartless and wae,
Sighing and moaning on ilka green loaning
The flowers of the forest are all wede away.'

HE Court was now established at Stirling, and a very dull and melancholy Court it was. The visit at Wemyss Castle had indeed borne ample fruit, but as if there was some fatality hanging over Mary Stuart's head, the days of courtship which, with most women, form such a happy era in life, were fraught for her with much annoyance, vexation, and distress. Though she had listened coyly at first to her handsome young suitor, she had not prohibited him from broaching the agreeable subject again, and by the beginning of April Lord Darnley was known to the whole of Scotland as the accepted lover of the Queen. It is needless to dwell upon the confusion created by such an announcement at the different Courts of Europe where her marriage had been made the subject of endless intrigue and diplomacy, nor the access of ill-humour which it produced in Elizabeth, who could never make up her mind as to the exact manner in which she should treat her Cousin. Cecil was sharply reproved for not having earlier fore-

seen so probable a contingency; Randolph received a rap over the knuckles for his tardiness in forwarding the disagreeable intelligence; and Lady Lennox, for no graver offence than that of being Darnley's mother, was committed to the Tower.

In Scotland the popular opinion was in favour of the match, although the vulgar, with their usual love for the marvellous, affirmed that their Queen's affections had been gained by magic arts; the favourite rumour being that Darnley had presented Her Majesty with an enchanted bracelet, made by the famous sorcerer, Lord Ruthven, who had shut himself up fasting for nine days and nights for the purpose, and finished it off in so short a space of time with no assistance but that of the arch fiend, his fellow-workman.

The spell, however, which the lover had cast upon his Mistress was probably stronger than anything likely to result from the black art, originating as it did in beauty of person, charm of manner, and above all the sympathetic attraction of young blood. That they had plighted their troth to one another was only to be presumed from the intimacy the Queen permitted him, and the obvious delight she experienced in his society.

Randolph was puzzled. He was fain to have some certain intelligence to convey to Cecil, and, although he had thoroughly sounded Mary Beton, who was beginning to get tired of attentions which never became more definite, he suffered no opportunity to escape him of watching the affianced pair.

The Court, we have said, was dull and melancholy. Darnley, stretched on a sick bed with an attack of measles, was sedulously tended by the Queen. His illness shed a gloom over the royal household, and Randolph was nearly satisfied in his own mind that the marriage was as good as concluded. He resolved, nevertheless, to place his suspicions beyond a doubt.

It was a sunshiny day in April, and the diplomatist knew that he was likely to see mistress Beton on the southern terrace of the Castle about noon. He awaited her there accordingly with a great affectation of anxiety and agitation. The lady, on the contrary, looked three inches taller than usual, and was as cold as ice.

'I have longed to see you, fair madam,' said the courtly gentleman; 'there is no sunshine for me where mistress Beton is not, and I pine like some tropical bird for the reviving warmth of her smiles.'

The comparison seemed a little ridiculous, as she contemplated 'the bird,' dressed with scrupulous attention, in the extremity of the mode, and wearing an enormous ruff. She smiled somewhat scornfully as she replied,

'You seem to keep your plumage marvellously sleek in the shade.'

'The bird seeks its mate,' answered he, laughing good-humouredly, 'and the two-legged creatures here below, like the fowls of heaven, always wear their gaudiest feathers in the pairing season. Mistress Beton, the cage door is open at last, and you are now free. Is it not so?'

He took her hand while he spoke, and pressed it warmly, but she released it with an impatient gesture, and answered angrily,

'What mean you, master Randolph? My freedom is not dependent upon *you*, I trow; nor do I see in what manner it concerneth you. I pray you, sir, let go my hand!'

'Nay, but is it not true that the Queen-bird hath chosen her mate?' he proceeded affectionately, and determined not to be affronted, at least not yet. 'In plain English, or rather in your pretty Scotch, tell me truth, fair mistress Beton, this Queen of yours hath given her consent to her kinsman, and the maidens are released from their vow?'

'I am not here to tell my Mistress's secrets,' answered the lady, none the less severely that her conscience reminded her she had not always been so discreet; 'surely master Randolph can get information more reliable than mine, or he hath indeed lived in ignorance for long!'

She was thinking that he had of late neglected her shamefully, but although his quick ear detected much of pique in her tone, there was so little affection in it, that he determined to alter his tactics, but warily, of course, and by degrees.

'You are offended with me, mistress Beton,' said he, in a quiet mournful voice, 'and therefore you are pitiless. Well, you will know better hereafter, perhaps when it is too late. I have but remained at this Court for the sake of others, and now it is time that I was gone. You must yourself know that my position here has been a false and delicate one: I am looked on coldly by your Queen; I am an object of jealousy and distrust to this new favourite of hers; I am continually reproached by my own employers for betraying too strong a bias towards the Scottish interest; and, worse than all, those whose good opinion I most value, and for whose sake I have lost so much, turn upon me at the last, and seem determined to fall out with me, whether I will or no. But it takes two to make a quarrel, mistress Beton, and I am resolved not to be one. Farewell! we part friends. Is it not so?'

A woman could hardly resist such an appeal from a man whom she had once cared for, if ever so little. She gave him her hand frankly, of her own accord this time, and murmured a few commonplace expressions of leave-taking and good will.

Randolph bowed over the hand he held, and drew a rare jewel from his doublet.

'You will accept this from me as a keepsake,' said he, coldly and courteously; 'perhaps you will look on it sometimes, and think of me more kindly when I am gone.'

It was a large gold locket, in the form of a heart, suspended from two clasped hands, richly ornamented with precious stones, and of a peculiar and fanciful device. Mary Beton started when she set eyes on it.

'Where did you get that?' she exclaimed, completely thrown off her guard. 'It belongs to the Queen!'

Randolph owned one peculiarity: he never smiled when he was really pleased, but had a trick of half shutting his eyes when he considered he had the best of the game; he looked as if he held a trump card now, while he answered quietly,

'That is surely mine own which I have fairly won. Lord Darnley paid me with that trinket in lieu of the fifty gold pieces he lost, when you and I beat Her Majesty and himself so handsomely at billiards the day before he was taken ill. I never thought the House of Lennox was overburdened with money, yet I can hardly believe its fortunes are at so low an ebb, that its heir must pay his debts with his love tokens.'

'It *is* so, nevertheless,' said Mary Beton, indignantly. 'It was the Queen's locket, and I saw her give it him with loving words, a thousand times more precious than the gift. Out upon him! a false knight! a recreant! I would have pawned my doublet first!'

Randolph had learned all he wanted to know. With a few kind phrases he soon took his leave of his companion, hurrying off, we may be sure, to convey the result of his enquiries without delay to his Court. It was not till he had been gone several minutes that Mary Beton cooled down sufficiently to reflect how indiscreetly she had suffered herself to be surprised, and how very unsatisfactory had been hitherto her dealings and relations with the English Ambassador.

The Maries were indeed all in trouble now, more or less. Here was their leader, the lady who expected them to look up to her for counsel and example, awaking to a sensation the most galling perhaps that can be experienced by the female heart—that of having been cozened out of its affections by one who has given nothing in return. In one way or another, we all of us go on playing silver against gold all our lives through, but it is not in human nature to have this humiliating truth thrust upon its notice, without vexation. Mary Beton fairly ground her white teeth together when she thought how near she had been to loving Mr. Randolph very devotedly, and how that astute gentleman had been making a cat's-paw of her all through, never so much as burning the tips of his own fingers the while. It was an aggravation to reflect on Ogilvy's honest nature, and the sincere homage she had spurned for the sake of one so much inferior in every manly quality to the frank-hearted soldier. And now Ogilvy was absent from the Court, and perhaps consoling himself for her unkindness in the smiles of another. Well, he would come back again, and it would go hard but she would resume her sway, if once she turned her mind to it, and was really determined to try.

A woman's spirit is tolerably elastic. We may say of it as Horace says of the shipwrecked merchant, '*mox reficit rates;*'—the bark may have had awful weather to encounter, have lost spars, and masts, and tackle by the fathom, perhaps damaged her screw, and sustained one or two very awkward bumps against a shoal—never say die! she puts in hopefully to refit, jury-masts are rigged, fresh canvass bent, leaks carefully stopped, and damages repaired; the first fine day she launches forth to sea again, almost as good as new.

But there are some exceptions that cannot thus recover, some natures to whom one keen disappointment of the affections is a moral death-blow; nay, there *are* rare cases in which such a wound is physically fatal. Mary Hamilton had never been like the same woman since Chastelâr's death. With a pale cheek and a languid step she went about her duties indeed as usual, but the light of her life seemed to be gone, and the only time a smile ever crossed that beautiful sad face was when, in the exercise of her devotions, the soul seemed to assert its superiority over the body, and to lift itself out of this earthly darkness into the 'everlasting day' beyond. Every one who came about Mary Hamilton seemed to acknowledge the refining influence of a spirit thus purified by suffering. The fiercest barons, the rudest men-at-arms felt softened and humanized while in her presence, and James Geddes the fool, after sitting gazing into her face for hours together, would break into a succession of such unearthly moans as subjected him to the discipline of the porter's lodge forthwith.

Lively mistress Seton was losing somewhat of her spirits and her elasticity. The laugh was no longer so frequent, though it might ring out at times as saucily as ever, and the step, though light and buoyant still, had acquired a more sober and regular tread as she went upon Her Majesty's errands through the gloomy passages of Stirling Castle. The young lady was learning to think. In her heart she did not thoroughly approve of this proposed match on which the Queen was now so bent, and considered Lord Darnley, with all his outward advantages and accomplishments, by no means good enough for her dear Mistress. Mary Seton had seen through him at once, as a woman often does, and detected under that fair outside the frivolous disposition, the reckless passions, and the utter want of heart beneath. If she had given her honest opinion, she would have said Bothwell was worth a dozen of him, and his big henchman, a hundred.

And what of Mary Carmichael? Proud, self-reliant, and undemonstrative, she was the last person on earth to have admitted that any anxiety or disappointment of her own could have deprived her cheek of one shade of colour, or dimmed her eye of one ray of brightness, and yet beautiful Mary Carmichael was losing day by day much of that brilliant freshness which had constituted no small portion of her beauty, and went about mournfully and in heaviness, as one who suffered keenly from some secret sorrow; yet the stranger who used to meet her in the garden at Holyrood had been seen at Stirling, and his clandestine interviews with the fair maid-of-honour had been of late more frequent than usual. If she was the happier for them, her appearance strangely belied her.

Yes, the Court was very dull now. Darnley was on a sick bed, and Mary and her maidens were in trouble, one and all.

CHAPTER XXXIV.

'"Fear ye nae that," quo' the laird's Jock,
"A faint heart ne'er won a fair ladie;
Work thou within, we'll work without,
And I'll be sworn we'll set thee free."'

UR worthy friend, 'Dick-o'-the-Cleugh,' seemed strangely altered as he rode back into Liddesdale. A moody man was Dick, and a silent; no longer the jovial comrade and 'devil-may-care' trooper that the other jack-men had heretofore known him, but a sulky and captious fellow-traveller, an abrupt and peremptory martinet. The borderer was beginning to find that he had a conscience, and to discover how unpleasant are the remonstrances of that monitor when displeased. His heart smote him sorely while he reflected on the part he had been compelled to play with regard to Maxwell, a man whose whole character had inspired him with admiration and respect, in whom also, as a constant frequenter of the Court, he took an affectionate interest that he did not care to analyse. And now he had lured this frank and friendly soldier into a trap from which it was doubtful if he would escape with life. The towers of Leslie were thick and lofty, and well guarded; the retainers of Rothes noted, like their chief, for an un-

scrupulous recklessness and defiance of all consequences. What chance for the naked prisoner in such a stronghold? Those damp and gloomy vaults could keep a secret well. It needed no outrage, neither steel nor poison, to silence an inmate for ever. The gaoler had but to forget a small black loaf, neglect to fill a shallow cruse of water, and who would ever chronicle the prisoner's agonies in a torturing, lingering death? 'Dick-o'-the-Cleugh' turned sick and faint at the thought.

He had ample leisure to indulge these painful fancies, for the rapidity with which Maxwell had been conveyed into Fife necessitated a slow return, even on the game powerful horses that carried the men-at-arms of Earl Bothwell. Ere the weary animals pricked their ears to welcome the towers of Hermitage, Dick had come to a resolution which neither discipline nor loyalty would have tempted him to abandon. His comrades, more astonished than irritated at the change in one whom they had been accustomed to consider the very pattern of a moss-trooper, shook their heads, and whispered one another that 'muckle Dick was *fey*,' signifying *doomed*, it being an old Scottish superstition that any sudden and complete change in the disposition of an individual denotes an early death. When Dick sat silent among the wassailers below the salt, and passed the black flagon untasted by, many a roistering associate looked a thought graver for the moment, as he pictured his old comrade stretched upon the heather, with the pale gleam of death upon his face, and a 'false Southron's' lance through his body, a thought graver, perhaps, for an instant, till a coarse jest or a fresh draught of ale brought him back to the gross and the material once more.

Hermitage Castle was no lightsome residence now. But for the return of military duties and the clang of arms at stated intervals in the court, it might have been a college or a monastery, so rarely was the voice of merriment heard within its walls. No more hawking and hunting now. The drawbridge had not been lowered, nor the portcullis raised, since Moray took his departure, with his solemn smile, following wild Rothes and his spearmen at half-a-day's interval, and leaving the Lord of the Castle in a mood of such stern and sullen defiance as caused the boldest of his retainers to shrink instinctively from his path. It seemed like another life that they used to lead long ago, dashing out in the dewy mornings with hawk on hand and hound at heel, or winding warily away in warlike order at set of sun for a moonlight foray on the southern side. The rude spearmen consoled themselves with great meals of beef and floods of ale, but the henchman's platter often remained untouched, his cup unfilled, whilst the Lord of the Castle himself, spent whole days of solitude in his own chamber, walking out at sunset to the northern rampart, where he would pace up and down for hours, far into the night.

His good angel had abandoned Bothwell at last, yet the spirit had left a gleam of its presence, a fragrance from its wings, about him still. Fast in the toils of unscrupulous Moray, the Earl could yet look back with a painful longing to the days when he was a loyal subject and a devoted knight to his beautiful Queen. At times he would be tempted to forego ambition, pride revenge, consistency, everything but his wild unreasoning affection, and, galloping to Holyrood or Stirling, fling himself at Mary's feet, entreat her to forgive him, and pledge himself, if it would make her happier, that he would never see her face again. Yes, there were moments when the proud strong man felt he would ask no more welcome relief than to bow his head and pour his heart out like a woman, in tears before his Queen; but then he thought of Darnley's youthful beauty, and Darnley's mocking smile, of the path that was still open to himself if he would crush all such foolish weaknesses, all such exaggerated notions of chivalry and forbearance. The fiend who is always at hand with his temptations, if a man gives him the least encouragement, whispered in his ear that *nothing* is impossible to one who has no scruples, and who will ungrudgingly risk all; that when honour, honesty, faith, and humanity are but rated as flimsy superstitions to bind weak intellects, and crime itself is considered simply as an untoward necessity or a decisive manœuvre, the will becomes all-in-all, and the master-spirit, that can *dare* boundlessly and unflinchingly, may aspire to the fulfilment of its boldest wishes and its wildest dreams. Bothwell, too, had been brought up in no precise or scrupulous school. In his adventurous career on the North Sea, many a scene of bloodshed and rapine had come under his notice, and one who had accustomed himself to direct those predatory descents on the Danish coast, which were but authorized acts of piracy after all, was not likely to entertain much compassion for a woman's shriek or a man's death-groan. It would have been no shrinking from bloodshed that could have deterred Bothwell from any scheme on which he had once thought well to enter.

Moray, too, had got the Earl completely in his hands. That wary statesman, in whom the *suaviter in modo* seems to have been admirably combined with the *fortiter in re*, had the peculiar faculty of acquiring unbounded influence over his associates, a power sometimes observable in the calm impassive nature, which never betrays its own feelings. Whatever might be the plot on which he was engaged, how high soever ran the waves through which the base-born Stuart steered his bark, not a shade of trepidation was to be detected on his quiet brow during its voyage, not a gleam of satisfaction when he had landed his cargo safely in port. It may be that men felt, so long as their interests were identical, they could *trust* Moray not to betray himself nor them. It may be that, though sadly warped to evil, his was a superior nature, born to command. Whatever was the cause, no intriguer could be more plausible, no party-leader more successful.

And Bothwell, eager, hot-headed, vain, perhaps even romantic, was a mere child in the hands of such a man as this. What could avail the bluff straightforward courage of the swordsman against the diplomatic *finesse* of the equally bold but far more subtle statesman? It was the old story of the long sweeping sabre against the delicate rapier, skilfully handled. The broad blade whistles through the air with mighty strokes that would serve to cleave a head-piece or to lop a limb, but ere it can descend amain, the thin line of quivering steel has wound its sinuous way under the guard and through the joints of the harness, and is drinking the streams of life-blood from the heart. Earl Bothwell was bound hand-and-foot to the half-brother of his Queen.

All these intrigues and vexations goaded the Warden to the verge of madness. He could scarce bear to be noticed, much less addressed by his retainers, and it was with a fierce oath and a savage glare that he accosted his henchman when the latter ventured to interrupt his solitary walk, one summer's evening, on the northern rampart.

The stars were coming out one by one in the soft twilight sky, and the Warden paced moodily to and fro, looking ever and anon wistfully towards the North.

'What lack ye man, in the fiend's name!' exclaimed the Earl, angrily. 'Must every knave that clears a trencher come into my presence unbidden? Silence, varlet, and begone!'

But Dick, too, had a sore heart and a perplexed brain, a combination which renders a man somewhat careless of outward observances. He was not to be daunted, even by the displeasure of his Chief, and he answered doggedly in return,

'I'll no be silent when it's for the Laird's honour that I suld speak! Oh! Bothwell, man, me an' mine has served you an' yours ever sin' Scotland was a kingdom, I'm thinkin'. Will ye no hear me speak the day?'

Dick's voice shook when he alluded to his feudal services. Stern as the giant looked, he was hoarse and trembling with emotion. Something in the Warden's breast responded to the appeal of his retainer, and he answered with assumed impatience,

'Say your say, man, in the devil's name, who seems

to be commanding officer here; out with your report, if report it be, and have done with it.'

'I wad wage my life for you, Bothwell, and that ye ken fine,' replied Dick, with something almost like tears shining in his eyes. 'I wadna grudge to shed every drap of bluid I hae, just to keep ye frae watting your foot. It's no danger, an' it's no disgrace, an' it's no death that wad daunton *me*, frae doing the Laird's bidding. No, no, 'Dick-o'-the-Cleugh' and Dick's forbears ha' eaten the Hepburn's bread and drunk frae the Hepburn's cup ower lang for the like o' that. But its just rackin' my heart to think o' yon lad in the donjon-keep at Leslie, and him breakin' bread in the Hepburn's hall and settin' his trust on the Hepburn's honour. And to think o' the like o' me pittin' his feet in the fetters and his craig in a tow; I wish my hands had rotted off at the elbows first!'

'What would you have, man?' said his Chief, somewhat less impatiently than the henchman had expected. ''Tis a mettled gallant, I grant ye, and a far-off kinsman of my own. What then? A soldier must take his chance; 'tis but the fortune of war.'

'' An' whan the leddies speir for their messenger at Holyrood, an' the bonny Queen hersel cries "Ou, he's safe eneugh, I trusted him to Bothwell;" how will we look if ever we come lilting into the Abbey-yard and can give no tidings of our guest?'

The Warden's brow softened, although he seemed considerably perplexed.

'I would he were safe back again, Dick,' replied he, 'I care not who knows it; but Rothes has a firm grip, and he would like well to make favour with Moray, even though he should disoblige *me*. I wish poor Walter may not be in a prison from which there is no breaking, at this present speaking. Aye! Dick, times are changed since my father's day. Earl Patrick, now, if he had wanted anything from the proudest baron in Scotland, would have gone and taken it with a hundred riders at his back.'

Dick snapped his fingers in great glee. He was reading his Chieftain's thoughts as he would have read the track of a herd of cattle driven but yesterday into Cumberland.

'It wadna tak' a hundred men,' said he, exultingly, 'to lift the plenishing of Leslie Hoos itsel', though it were garrisoned with a' the loons in Fife. I wad but ask for Ralph Armstrong and 'Lang Willie,' an' maybe Little 'Jock-o'-the-Hope,' to bring awa' maister Maxwell in a whole skin, gin he lay in the heart o' Carlisle gaol!'

'It might not be a bad ploy for some of our lads,' answered Bothwell, with rather a fierce smile. 'Horses get fat and men lazy, cooped up here within four grey walls, and I might require man and horse in proper trim before long. Hark ye, Dick, if ye want to go northward for some ten days or so, I shall not ask ye where ye have been at your return. No thanks! leave me, man! If it come to blows, that long body o' yours can take care of itself.'

For the next hour or two 'Dick-o'-the-Cleugh' looked like a different person as he busied himself preparing man and horse for a march that he determined should commence at night-fall. When the sun had set, and the Earl, after deeper potations than ordinary, had retired from his habitual walk on the rampart, his henchman and three companions rode steadily out of the Castle-yard followed by many enquiring looks from their comrades, who, heartily wearied of their forced inaction, beheld with strong feelings of envy the departure of the little cavalcade. It consisted but of four individuals, nevertheless it would have been difficult among all Lord Bothwell's retainers to have selected a more efficient-looking *quartette*. With the exception of 'Dick-o'-the-Cleugh' himself, Ralph Armstrong was esteemed the most powerful man in Liddesdale; he was a stolid-looking fellow too, with considerable mother-wit concealed under a composure that nothing could ruffle, and a courage that nothing could daunt. 'Lang Willie,' again, was an exceedingly voluble and amusing companion, chiefly distinguished for his extraordinary skill as a swordsman, and the readiness and coarseness of his repartees. 'Little Jock-o'-the-Hope,' so called simply because he was the youngest of the party, was an active, limber, powerful fellow with all the mettle of his twenty summers and the sagacity of twice his age.

With such a following, and a moonless night in his favour, Dick would have been nothing loth to lay a wager that he would cross the Southern Border, and take Lord Scrope by the beard.

They rode all night merrily enough; steadily though, and careful not to distress their horses. As they neared the capital Dick's spirits rose visibly, and his comrades could not but remark on his resumption of his old habits of good-fellowship; but at daybreak an incident occurred which cast a gloom over the henchman's superstitious nature, and plunged him once more into that gloomy taciturnity which was so foreign to his real disposition.

It was in the grey of the dawn. Dick was riding at the head of the party, who followed in single file, for the track lay through some boggy and broken ground in which two horses could not go abreast. Suddenly a hare that had been cropping the dank herbage thus early stole into the path in front of them, and leaped slowly along under the very nose of the henchman's charger. This, although an untoward omen, was too common an occurrence to create alarm. There was an established *formula* for all such cases made and provided. Though too good a Protestant to cross himself, Dick repeated the customary charm with edifying gravity; but as though in defiance the hare still kept on in front of them. At three different angles in the path she hesitated, seeming about to turn off to right or left, and then hopped slowly on in the direction they were travelling. The stout borderers grew pale. It was even proposed that they should retrace their steps and abandon the enterprise; but Dick suggested that as he was the person immediately in front, his must be the entire risk, and the warning must be especially intended for him. The others were well satisfied to take this view of the matter, and presently they were discoursing as blithely as before; but their leader felt a depression of spirits creeping over him which he strove in vain to overcome, and as the gloom gathered darker and darker about him, he felt in the depths of his rude nature that presentiment of coming death which, let philosophers say what they will, is no unusual precursor of the final catastrophe.

His past life comes back to him with strange vividness as he rides silently on. His father's rude grey tower at the head of the glen; the sunny, grassy nook where he used to play by the shallow burn with five sturdy urchins like himself, and one golden-haired brother whom they missed at last from amongst them, and told each other in awed whispers, looking up at the sky the while, how 'Willie was gone to heaven.' Till to-day he had almost forgotten the gleam of his father's broad-sword, and the caresses of a gentle care-worn woman who used to hush him to sleep with low plaintive songs. He remembers, too, with peculiar distinctness, that first ride on the tall bay gelding, and the mimic lance with which he drove his imaginary foray.

These early memories are clearer to him now than many a real scene of plunder and bloodshed in which he knows he has since taken too much delight, but his devotion to his Chief is as intense as ever, albeit dashed with something of a melancholy tenderness that seems unnatural, and derogatory to both.

Another figure, too, comes flitting across the borderer's mental sight; a figure that is seldom long absent from his dreams either by day or night; a figure that he dares to dwell on now for the first time these long weeks past without shame, because he feels that he is about to vindicate his loyalty to all belonging to her or to her Queen.

He can almost hear the ringing tones of her voice,

can almost catch the flutter of her dress. Surely he is bewitched! bewitched or else irrevocably doomed to death. As he gathers a sprig of witch-elm and fastens it in his morion, he says to himself that if he is really to die, he should like to see Mary Seton just once again.

CHAPTER XXXV.

'For this is love, and this alone,
   Not counting cost nor grudging gain,
That builds its life into a throne,
   And bids the idol reign;

'That hopes and fears, yet seldom pleads,
   And for a sorrow weakly borne,
(Because it yields not words but deeds)
   Can hide a gentle scorn;

'In pride and pique that takes no part,
   Of self and sin that bears no taint,
The homage of a knightly heart
   For a woman and a saint.'

HE four borderers rode up the High-street of Edinburgh in the warm afternoon sun, and their leader, fortified doubtless by the sprig of witch-elm in his head-piece, and inspirited by his arrival at the Scotch capital, looked about him with the gleeful curiosity of a school-boy on a holiday.

On any other occasion, though troops of armed horsemen were by no means a rare sight on the causeway, so well mounted and stalwart a little party would have received their share of admiration, but to-day no man had eyes to spare for any other object than a brilliant group of foot-passengers surrounding two commanding figures, which neither their own nor any other country in Europe could have matched.

No more in widow's weeds, but bright and beautiful in all the freshness of her own charms, set off by the splendour of her dress, Mary Stuart walked by her young husband, the *beau idéal* of a Monarch's bride. Her husband *de facto* if not *de jure*, for a private marriage some weeks since in Riccio's apartments had united the destinies of the lovers, and paved the way for that public ceremony which should confer on the fortunate young noble the crown-matrimonial of Scotland.

Alas for Mary Stuart! even in those happy days of courtship, which for most women glow so brightly, immediately before and after the nuptial tie she was doomed to many anxieties and misgivings, originating in the ungovernable temper of the very man for whose sake she had braved Elizabeth of England's displeasure, affronted a large and powerful party of her subjects, perhaps even stifled and eradicated certain deep though unacknowledged memories in her own heart. Although with the utmost haste Darnley had been created Earl of Ross, he was dissatisfied that he had not been immediately raised to the Dukedom of Albany, and vented his displeasure in no measured language even on her from whose open hand he received all the benefits he enjoyed, and whose beauty alone, bending so tenderly over himself, should have commanded his entire allegiance.

Perhaps the Queen loved him none the worse for his petulance at first; perhaps it was not till long afterwards, when unlimited indulgence and increasing depravity had fostered the spoiled and wayward youth into a reckless and unfeeling profligate, that she may have contrasted Darnley's open insults and avowed indifference with the devotion of other worshippers, who, however faulty in many respects, had never failed in faith and loyalty towards *her*.

Darnley's exterior was indeed beautiful exceedingly, but it covered a disposition in which there were no brilliant qualities of the head to counterbalance the evil of the heart. The Earl of Ross was unfortunate in the possession of dishonesty without craft, indecision without foresight, and obstinacy without energy. Like a woman, he could not restrain his tongue; unlike a woman, he never knew the exact range and precision with which that organ is able to direct its shafts.

Even on his sick bed at Stirling, when it was first obvious to him that he had won his way into his Sovereign's good graces, and that a little time and care could not but make the game his own; even then, when it was essentially important to cement friendships and conciliate differences in every direction, he contrived to affront the two most formidable men in Scotland and purchase their enmity for life; to the Duke of Chatelhérault, simply because he heard that nobleman was opposed to Her Majesty's immediate marriage, he sent his defiance from his sick-bed, not couched in the language of knightly courtesy which shows a gracious respect even for a mortal foe, but threatening to 'knock his old pate as soon as he should be well enough.'

We may imagine how such a message would be

received by one who boasted he was the proudest peer in Europe. But an observation he made concerning the Earl Moray, and which did not fail to reach the latter's ears, was even more ill-advised in its tendency and unfortunate in its results.

Scanning a map of Scotland, some one pointed out to him the vast estates of the Queen's half-brother, and the inconsiderate youth exclaimed hastily,

'This is too much by half!'

So untoward a remark was of course repeated to Moray, who received the information with his usual grave smile, and never made further allusion to it. So much the worse. He had forgotten it none the less for that, and it may be those half-dozen words one day cost Mary Stuart a husband and Scotland a king.

Meantime who so brave in apparel or so *debonair* in demeanour as the young Lord Darnley? The eyes of all Edinburgh are upon him as he paces along so proudly by the side of their 'bonny Queen.' His dress, as it is fit, is one blaze of splendour; the materials indeed are unpaid for, and the jewels are mostly love-gifts from his Sovereign, yet they set off none the worse his lofty stature and his graceful form. The women look after him admiringly, the men's gaze is as usual riveted on the beautiful being who walks by his side. Mary Stuart has never shown to more advantage than to-day. It is not the stately folds of the damask dress, nor the delicate edging of scalloped lace, nor the rich mantle of glowing *cramoisie* that enthral the eyes in an irresistible spell; nor needs it that massive bracelet hanging from her shapely arm, which men say dark Lord Ruthven fabricated for a love-charm, with Satan standing over him while he worked, to account for Mary's influence; they need but to look on the bright smile and the deep loving eyes turned in pride and tenderness upon her husband, and they feel in their inmost hearts that there is no witchery in all the lore of gramarye to equal the resistless power that lurks in a fond and trusting woman's face.

Darnley has turned back for an instant to exchange some light jest with one of the maids-of-honour; it must be of a strangely confusing nature to account for the vivid blush that has come over Mary Seton, dying her fair skin perfectly crimson from the roots of her hair to the hem of her boddice. 'Dick-o'-the-Cleugh' riding up the street and watching intently the motions of the royal party, does not perceive it for the simple and somewhat paradoxical reason that, although he has been hoping to see her the whole way from Hermitage, no sooner has he caught her eye than his own glance is immediately withdrawn. He turns deadly pale too, and the hand which guides his charger's rein trembles in every fibre; the good horse bends his neck and collects himself, expectant of some further indication after this unusual touch.

Perhaps poor Dick, with all his courage, might have ridden on into Fife without more parley, so helpless and abashed had he suddenly become, but that the Queen's quick glance observed the cognizance of the Hepburn as he rode by, even recognised the tall retainer's face, and could have accosted him by name. There was a faint flush on Mary's brow as she stopped her company and bade the borderer approach. Dick was off his horse in an instant, and the courtiers could not but admire his magnificent form as he strode up to them in his clanging armour, manning himself for the effort, now he was in for it, with his natural audacity. Mary Seton did not fail to remark, with no displeased eye, that even Darnley, tall as he was, stood half a hand's-breadth lower than the henchman.

'What news from Hermitage, good fellow?' said the Queen, accepting Dick's awkward homage with gracious courtesy. 'How fares it with our Lord Warden yonder on the Marches? Mayhap he is coming northward with the main body, of which you are but the van-guard?'

She spoke with something of flutter and hurry that was scarce natural to her. Perhaps she wished the retainer to know that she bore his sullen lord no ill-will; perhaps she even expected her vassal to return to her feet in penitence and contrition; perhaps, in her woman's heart, even now she could not but revert to the old times, when Bothwell's haste regarded neither pace nor horse-flesh to gallop on far a-head of his following, only to be the first to kneel at his Queen's feet and touch the hem of her garment.

Dick answered stoutly though in some confusion,

'The Laird's no ailing in body, your Grace, though he wad be nane the waur to be whiles in the saddle a wee thing. The Hepburn's feet aye become steel stirrups better than velvet mules.* He's less wise-like than ordinar',' added Dick, with a shrewd glance in

---

* Slippers.

Her Majesty's face; 'but I'm thinkin' he'll bide in Liddesdale a whiley yet.'

Mary laughed good-humouredly. It did not seem to displease her that Bothwell should be sullen and dispirited. Yet she bore him no grudge for it, obviously; rather the contrary.

'The Liddesdale lads are aye welcome at Holyrood,' said she frankly, and with the Scottish accent she knew how to assume so gracefully; 'take a Stuart's word for it,' she added, giving him at the same time her hand to kiss, 'both for yourself and your Chief.'

'Dick-o'-the-Cleugh' kissed the beautiful hand with the devotion of a worshipper to a saint; but his eyes wandered beyond the royal form and sought that of a lady in her train.

At this moment Darnley came up from behind and accosted the henchman with his usual overbearing assumption of manner.'

'How now, whom have we here, my fair cousin?' said the young noble, flinging a contemptuous glance at the borderer. 'An ambassador from Limbo Castle, sometimes called Hermitage, by his crest! Accredited messenger from all the thieves and sorners in the Debateable Land. How ranges the price of good nags on the Border, knave? The nights are moonless just now, though they be something short; the droves should be coming in pretty fast from Cumberland.'

The moss-trooper's eye brightened.

'If it was Her Grace's wish,' said he, looking respectfully towards the Queen, 'we could bring the wale* o'

---

* Pick.

the country-side up to Holyrood in a fortnight from this day. Lord Scrope rides a soar gelding,' he added, warming with the congenial subject, ' that steps as daintily as a bird lights on a bough. Forbye the colour would become rarely Her Grace's housings and foot-mantle. If I might make so bold, I wad engage he should be in Her Majesty's stable or he was weel missed at Warkworth. I wad send ain o' my lads back for him this very night!'

Darnley burst into a loud mocking laugh.

'A thorough moss-trooper,' he exclaimed, ' rider, jack-man, plunderer, thief, call them what you will, they are all alike; fit followers of such a Chief. Were I King of Scotland I would have the halters off the horses and put them on the men, string them up in rows with this tall knave at their head, not forgetting his worthy master, the leader of the gang.'

The young man spoke in laughing boisterous accents that might be taken either for jest or earnest, but the borderer's face flushed dark-red, and the fingers of his left hand closed like a vice upon his sheathed sword.

'If ever you *are* King of Scotland,' said he, ' may ye die no less noble a death than him who lay by the Till, yon summer's evening, with the proudest and the bauldest an' the best down about him like trees felled in a rank, and wha but the borderers sleepin' man by man at gentle King James's feet! It sets a Scottish lord ill to speak again' them that keeps the Scottish line, an' warst of all a limber lad like your Honour, (no offence to ye,) that's got soldier written on his brow, and swordsman marked on every yane o' his lang limbs.'

The compliment to his personal appearance, always an acceptable offering to Darnley, modified whatever he might have considered offensive in the henchman's plain-speaking. The Queen, too, who had listened to the colloquy with obvious displeasure and some uneasiness, now laid her hand on the arm of her consort and motioned him to proceed with their walk. The latter felt in his girdle for a couple of gold pieces, which were not however forth-coming, then with a careless laugh and a whisper in Riccio's ear, nodded insolently to the borderer, and passed on with Mary and her train.

One of these, however, lingered a few paces in the rear. Dick's face grew very pale once more when mistress Seton turned back and accosted him with her own bright glance and her own merry smile.

'You are slow of speech,' said she, 'I know of old, though prompt in deed, and as true as the steel in your belt. Is it not so?'

His lips were white and dry. He could not answer in words, but his affirmative gesture was more convincing than a hundred oaths.

She laid her hand on his. Through the steel gauntlet that light touch thrilled in every vein and fibre of the giant.

'You will tell me the truth,' she proceeded. 'What of Walter Maxwell? We have had no tidings of him since the morning he rode away from Holyrood, weeks and months ago!'

It speaks well for Mary Seton's good-nature that the subject uppermost in her mind was one which she believed so vitally affected the welfare of her friend. It was as much kindliness of disposition as female curiosity that riveted her attention on the borderer's reply.

Dick's face became a study of self-reproach and embarrassment while he related the treachery of which Walter had been the victim; neither concealing nor palliating his own share in the business, which seemed to himself the less black that it was taken in compliance with his Chief's orders, and for which his listener either forgot or neglected to reprove him. It is impossible to take the same interest in other people's matters that we do in our own, and what a world of confusion we should have if the confidants and go-betweens in a love-affair were as much agitated as the principals.

Mary Seton heard him calmly enough, and then proceeded to interrogate him about Bothwell. The henchman's answers concerning his Chief seemed to afford her matter both of surprise and gratification. The Earl was evidently in a state of discomfort and restlessness that must be reported at once to the Queen, who had always betrayed extraordinary interest in everything connected with Hermitage or the Borders, and his rude follower seemed to have observed and analysed his feelings with a sagacity that must have been strangely sharpened by some influence from without.

If there was a more triumphant sparkle in Mary Seton's eye, a tinge of deeper colour on her cheek, as she reflected on the nature of that influence, who shall blame her? Was she not a woman; and is it not a woman's instinct, like a cat's, to tease and tantalize her prey to the utmost? Though the mouse be as big as an elephant, it is such fun to tempt him with the prospect of indulgence, or even liberty, and then sweep him irresistibly back again with one stroke of the cruel velvet paw.

Mary Seton smiled within herself and felt twice as big as the great borderer trembling there before her. With a whole budget of news gained for her Sovereign, she reverted to the topic most interesting to her comrade.

'You think then that he is alive, though in close ward?' she asked. 'They are cruel folk, I have heard say, the "lightsome Leslies." I would poor Walter were safe out of their hands!'

Dick had found his voice at last,

'And safe he shall be!' was his reply, 'before another week has passed over his head. It may tak' time, an' it may tak' skill, an' it may tak' twa or three men's lives, but we'll ha maister Maxwell, oot 'gin we ding doun Leslie itsel', an' mak' a low* that'll light up the twa Lomonds and the tae half o' the kingdom of Fife! That's what I'm here for now.'

She looked at him archly,

'Was that all that brought you to Edinburgh?' said she.

Again something seemed to choke the man-at-arms and prevent his reply. At last he spoke in a hoarse whisper,

'I was fain to see the Court once more—and the Queen—and—and—yersel', mistress Seton! I'll no win back to Liddesdale I'm thinkin'. But I'll tak' the

* Flame.

brunt o' it bra' an' easy the noo, sin' I've seen ye to wish ye farewell.'

Something in his tone so tender, so hopeless, and so respectful, touched the girl to the heart. She laid her hand once more in his, and he wrung it hard in his own strong fingers, but did not even presume to put it to his lips. Only as she turned away to join the Queen, a low stifled sob smote upon her ear, and looking back she beheld the borderer standing as if spell-bound on the spot where she had left him. The next moment he was in the saddle, and as he passed her moving up the street after the others, he detached the sprig of witch-elm from his morion and cast it at her feet, ere he galloped off.

Mary Seton's eyes filled with tears while she picked it up, and Dick's honest heart would have leapt with joy, notwithstanding his forebodings, could he have seen her hide it away carefully and tenderly in her bosom. When she rejoined the royal party, Riccio's sharp countenance wore a look of curiosity, for his quick eye detected that she had been weeping, but the Queen called her to her side, and soothed and caressed her, speaking in gentle loving tones like a mother to a child.

CHAPTER XXXVI.

'Oh! Espérance! Hope on! The fight
Is never lost while fight we may;
At home the hearth is shining bright,
Though yet unseen along the way;
And the darkest hour of all the night
Is that which brings us day.'

ONG weeks of solitary confinement in a dungeon, dark and damp and dismal, nourished on bread and water, and cheered only by the periodical visits of an asthmatic gaoler, appointed to that post because fit for nothing else, would destroy the courage of most men, as it would sap their bodily health and vigour. Walter Maxwell had need of all his strength of mind, all his natural qualities of bravery and endurance to resist the influence of his imprisonment, ere he had spent many weeks in the strong room of Leslie House. This place of confinement, paved and walled with stone, lighted by but one window, narrow and iron-barred, communicated with a winding staircase, and a long gloomy subterranean passage terminating in a wicket, which opened on a pleasaunce and flower garden. Prisoners might thus be smuggled in or out of the Leslie's stronghold without exciting observation; and unless the Lord of Rothes was

much belied, this facility of ingress was used for a variety of purposes, foreign to its original object. On summer evenings, 'tis said, the flutter of a farthingale might sometimes be seen emerging from its dark recesses, while lighter steps and merrier voices than were likely to belong to a permanent prisoner echoed in the damp underground passage leading in and out of Leslie House. Under these circumstances, bars were sometimes left undrawn and locks unturned, nor was Walter ignorant of the occasional negligence in which lay his only chance of escape.

The old gaoler, too, albeit short in temper as in wind, was not entirely destitute of compassion for a hungry and thirsty man. After the first fortnight and when he found that his Lord gave no orders for Maxwell to be starved to death, he brought him on rare occasions a morsel of venison or even a flask of wine, mollified as it would seem by the courage and good-humour with which his charge bore the rigours of captivity.

Then old Ralph, as he was called, would sometimes put down his pitcher and his keys to remain for a few minutes' conversation, or what he considered such, being indeed a monologue on his own grievances, his own infirmities, and, when in high good-humour, his youthful prowess and general accomplishments. These occasional visits were as beneficial to Maxwell's moral condition as the meat and wine were to his physical man.

After a week or two without exchanging a word with a fellow-creature, the stupidest of companions is welcomed like an angel from heaven, the dreariest

platitudes fall like spring showers upon a desert soil.
Maxwell *really* rejoiced in the visits of his gaoler,
looking forward to them as the sole events of his long,
uninteresting day, and old Ralph began to take a great
pride and pleasure in the prisoner who greeted him so
warmly, and showed himself such an accomplished
listener. By degrees the warder became confidential,
not to say indiscreet, though the last idea in his mind
was to favour his prisoner's escape. Indeed he could
not afford to part with him, and little by little
Maxwell, with his energies aroused and his intellects
sharpened by the emergency of his case, made himself familiar with the arrangements of the Castle, and
the details, of which he hoped to take advantage at
some future time.

The sensations of a prisoner enduring solitary confinement have been so often analysed and described,
that it is needless to enlarge upon them here. Without some distant hope of escape, without some definite
point for the mind to rest on, the infliction would
become unbearable, and end probably in insanity.
Maxwell, however, possessed one of those dogged,
resolute dispositions not uncommon amongst his countrymen, which, like iron at the forge, become only
harder and harder the more heavily they are struck.
From the first moment of his entrance, bound and
blindfolded into the Leslie's stronghold, he had determined to escape. That he was not to be put to
death he argued from the pains that had been taken
to kidnap him; and the knowledge that 'Dick-o'-the-Cleugh,' notwithstanding his apparent treachery, was
still his friend at heart, was a vague source of comfort

and re-assurance. The hours, marked only by the shadows on the blank and dreary wall, were indeed long—oh! so long! but the continued effort to keep mind and body in a condition to take advantage of any chance that might offer, served almost in lieu of an occupation and a pursuit.

The prisoner would force himself to pace the narrow limits of his cell for hours at a time, that he might not lose the wind and strength so necessary to that problematical flight which was the one fixed idea of his brain.

By degrees Walter observed that the precautions taken for his security became more and more relaxed. With all his senses sharpened by constant watching, he could hear the door at the foot of the winding-stair which led to the subterranean passage, although carefully locked at sundown, grating ajar on its hinges during the day, could detect the summer air stealing even to his remote dungeon, denoting that the door into the garden was also unfastened. By dint of constant attention he became satisfied at last that if he could but break out to the top of the stairs any time before night-fall during the summer afternoon, he might at least reach the garden without hindrance. Once there, though ignorant of the locality, he trusted to the chapter of accidents to make his escape into the open country beyond.

The first object was as far as possible to hood-wink Ralph, and that worthy's implicit confidence in the quiet demeanour of his charge would go far towards assisting him in his scheme; then, when the gaoler was thrown completely off his guard, a bold stroke would effect at least the first stage of the project. We do not affirm that the idea of springing on his keeper, who, although armed, might have been overpowered by a younger and stronger man, and beating out his brains with his own keys, did not present itself to Walter's mind, but such a measure was wholly repugnant to his character, and he resolved to attain freedom without shedding the blood of the old man who had mitigated, as far as he could, the rigour of his captivity.

By little and little the prisoner had discovered that no amount of outcry or disturbance in the dungeon could be heard without; of this he had satisfied himself by a series of experiments. This was always a step gained in the futherance of his plan.

Fortunately for himself also Maxwell was a large-boned man, especially in the wrists. Every set of fetters in the Castle had been successively tried on him and found too tight, so for a time he had been bound hand and foot with ropes; but on his complaining that these cut him, they had been withdrawn, and his limbs suffered to remain at liberty.

So all the fine summer days, when the June roses were blooming without, and the June grass growing, and the June birds singing on the tree, while within the rat and the spider were the only living creatures, and a green slime on the wall the only vegetable production, Maxwell was preparing his escape, and biding his time patiently for a favourable opportunity to put it in execution.

When Ralph used to bring his prisoner a draught of wine, he would sometimes, if in a particularly good-humour, condescend to stay for a few minutes and help him to partake of it. On these occasions Maxwell, by a studiously quiet and even languid demeanour, contrived to throw his gaoler completely off his guard.

One day he requested the wine might be left with him to cheer his solitude when his agreeable friend was gone; another time he complained of indisposition but thought he might relish a cup towards night-fall. By degrees he collected a Scottish pint or so of strong red wine in a stone jar that he had begged might be applied to the purpose.

The weather was very hot; even in a dungeon its inmate could tell that the summer-sun was glowing bright and fierce without. Old Ralph arrived according to custom with his prisoner's afternoon meal, and sat himself down on the stone floor like a man thoroughly overcome with his exertions.

'Take a draught of wine, man,' said Maxwell, pointing to the jar; ''tis the coolest place in the Castle here, and by St. Andrew the prisoner hath the best of it to-day.'

The old man smiled grimly; then he took a hearty pull as desired, and set the vessel down with a sigh of great satisfaction.

'An old man's bluid aye wants warmin',' said he, looking pensively into the vessel the while; 'but I've kent it far hotter ower sea. Whan I was in Flanders wi' Norman Leslie, ye ken;—aye! he was a wild lad, Norman, but a bra' soldier, fair sir, a bra' soldier as ever belted on a brand;—aweel, whan I was in Flanders wi' Norman ———,' and forthwith the old man embarked upon a long story of which gallant Norman Leslie was the hero, moistening his narrative at frequent intervals with draughts of the strong red wine, and Maxwell watched with strung nerves and beating heart, how his eye grew dimmer and his speech more laboured as the tale progressed and the contents of the vessel waned.

Nevertheless the door was locked on the inside, and the gaoler's fingers kept an instinctive grasp upon his keys. Once, catching Maxwell's eye fixed on these implements, he shifted them suddenly into the hand farthest from his prisoner, although in the act he interrupted himself in an elaborate description of a certain blue velvet surcoat, by which Norman Leslie set much store, and did not again recover the thread of his recollections until he had discovered that the wine was done and it was time for him to be gone.

But it was obviously necessary to lull his suspicions and induce him to remain a few minutes longer.

'I should like to hear how that surcoat was finished and embroidered,' said Maxwell, with an affectation of interest. 'The time of my release is drawing near,' he added, 'and when I go out I should wish to have one of the same colour and conceit.'

He spoke in so matter-of-fact a tone that old Ralph was thrown completely off his guard.

'Oot!' said he, 'it's the first time ever I heard it, lad. I'll no say but I'll miss ye! Oot! Gude presairve us! Was there ever the like o' that?'

'I told you when I came in,' replied his prisoner, yawning and stretching himself lazily the while, 'the full term will be out the day after to-morrow at noon.'

Old Ralph laid down his keys and scratched his head.

That instant Maxwell pounced upon them like a tiger. Almost with the same motion he seized the old man round the body completely pinioning him, heavy and powerful as he was, till he had sent him staggering to the farthest extremity of the cell. Then with one rapid turn of the key, that key at which he had often looked so longingly, and of which he knew every ward, he was through the door; as rapidly he locked and bolted it on the outside. His hand never trembled, his nerves were as true to him now in the moment of success, as they had been through all the dangers and disasters he had overcome.

'Ah!' thought Maxwell, as he sped down the winding-stair like a lapwing, 'you may holloa your heart out, as many a poor prisoner has done before, but nobody will come near you till supper-time. If you get not free for a week you'll have had a lighter captivity than mine. And now for liberty and life, and—Mary Carmichael!'

He believed he had schooled himself to think of her no more, but she came back to him with the first gleam of the summer sun, the first breath of the summer air.

There is no catastrophe of grief or discomfiture so staggering to the nervous system as the shock of a great relief or a great joy. You shall attend the sickbed of one nearest and dearest to you for days together, and see the life that is more precious than your very heart's blood ebbing away, as it were, inch by inch, and drop by drop, yet your eyes are dry, though your brain feels strangely hot and seared, your hand is steady, your tread firm, and your pulse regular. The moment on which hang the issues of life and eternity comes at last. The silent strife is waged between sleep and death, and the gentle conqueror triumphs by a hair's breadth. Never prone to give his opinion rashly, the doctor tells you that the dear one has escaped 'out of danger, he is happy to inform you,' and you wring his hand fiercely, but something griping at your throat forbids you to speak your thanks. Then, the tears gush freely to your eyes; then, the strong frame shakes and quivers in every fibre, and down upon your knees you kneel before your God, even if you never knelt before. So in all the relations of life, the moment of success is the touchstone to the human character. It is far more rare to find men bear prosperity with equanimity than adversity. We have all heard of people going mad for joy.

For an instant, Walter Maxwell had to pause and collect his energies, manning himself as though about to undergo some formidable trial, when he found he was at last on the *outside* of that door which he had contemplated such a weary while as the bar between himself and freedom. Stealthily, and with a keen sense of delight, so overpowering as to be almost painful, he pushed open the iron wicket at the foot of the staircase and emerged into the garden beyond.

It was intoxicating to drink in the warm fragrance of the summer air at every pore. It was bewildering, from sheer delight, to feel the eyes ache in that dazzling sunshine, glowing on leaf and flower, whitening the gravel walk and the castle wall in its blinding glare. The prisoner paused in a corner of the passage ere he came forth, accustoming sight and faculties by degrees to the rapturous change.

Then he stole out and looked about him, taking in, with keen and wary eye, the features of the surrounding scene. Well he knew that in such a stronghold as that of the powerful Rothes his escape had only just begun.

He found himself in a beautiful little garden, neatly kept and tastefully laid out. Casting a hasty glance upward he ascertained that he was overlooked by no windows from the Castle; three sides of this parterre were bounded by the great blank walls of the house, the fourth was shut in by a dark impervious hedge of yews. With stealthy hasty steps he was soon on the farther side of this leafy screen and traversing a bowling-green, on which the bowls, dotting the level surface at irregular intervals, denoted that a game had been recently interrupted, he emerged upon a beautiful little wilderness of shrubs and flowers beyond.

Three or four vases and a fountain adorned this exterior pleasure ground, and the gigantic beeches of Leslie, perhaps the finest trees in Scotland, shaded it with their dark gleaming foliage. It looked like a paradise to the emancipated prisoner; but alas, a paradise from which there was no escape. Surrounded by the outer wall of the Castle, any biped, unprovided with wings, seemed as much a captive in those sunny glades as in the darkest recesses of the dungeon. How Maxwell envied the butterfly soaring into the air so freely over that smooth and cruel wall. It would be hard to turn back now after tasting even for five minutes the delights of liberty.

Casting about with anxious eyes and a fast beating heart for some means, however desperate, of egress, he espied a portion of the masonry in which certain irregularities would admit of his climbing to within a few feet of the coping. At this very place, too, a friendly beech somewhat overhung the garden so that one of its branches drooped downwards inside the wall.

With a run and a bound, like that of a wild cat, he swarmed up its slippery surface and succeeded in reaching the pendant branch. It was a desperate exertion of strength, and the pain that shot across his chest warned Maxwell how an ounce more of weight would have turned the scale in the effort by which he swung himself into the tree. Once there, he paused to take breath, and looked back into the garden from which he had so happily escaped. What was his dismay to observe, for the first time, a tall stalwart man, in the guise of a labourer, shuffling into his jerkin and making for the house!

'Of course,' thought Maxwell, with a curse on his own stupidity that he had not perceived the man sooner, 'to give the alarm and turn out the retainers for pursuit!'

In truth there was nothing for it now but to slip down from the tree and trust to a light pair of heels and the chapter of accidents.

Already his legs were clear of the branches and he was meditating a drop of some four or five yards upon the sward, when he drew them up again with wondrous precipitation, for the tread of feet through the grass, and the sound of voices in earnest conclave, warned him that he was hemmed in and beset on this side as well as the other.

Close under the tree, in which he couched like some

hunted animal, three gallants halted, and carried on their conversation in the deep, low, earnest tones of men who discuss those matters on which they have bound themselves to secrecy, and which the bird of the air itself is not to overhear.

Splendidly dressed, although half-armed, for a Scottish noble loved not to be utterly defenceless, even in the heart of his own residence and the company of his staunchest friends, Maxwell recognised them at once, for three of the most powerful men in the kingdom—the wariest of statesmen, the darkest of intriguers, the most reckless of conspirators.

Not one of the three would have scrupled to cut the throat of an unwelcome eaves-dropper on the spot, whether or no he thought a word of their conversation was overheard or understood. That 'makin sicker' has been a favourite expedient in the annals of our northern politicians ever since Kirkpatrick left the red Comyn weltering in his blood on the steps of the altar.

It was an unpleasant predicament for poor Walter. What could he do but hide himself up among the branches, keep quiet and listen, expecting besides every moment that the alarm of his escape would be given from the Castle?

The little conclave continued their conversation eagerly, and as they stood beneath his hiding-place, Maxwell had ample leisure to observe the faces and bearing of his Queen's three worst and most pitiless enemies.

Rothes was as usual gay and careless in demeanour; his handsome face, flushed with wine, was not out of keeping with the disordered bravery of his apparel. He could break his jest on treason as on any other crime; could pass through life and its most important avocations as though it were but one long feverish debauch in which the merriest and wildest roisterer bore his part the best.

Argyle, who repressed his host's ill-timed mirth whenever opportunity offered, and listened attentively to the calm measured accents of the third person present, seemed thoughtful and ill-at-ease.

Though of a courageous character, his was a nature that weighs well every scheme on which it enters, and loves not to put forth its full powers unless it sees its way clearly to success. He could not go hand over head into a plot like Rothes simply for the excitement and amusement of the turmoil.

Grave in demeanour as the man to whom he was now listening so attentively, and not unlike him in character, he was yet far inferior in foresight and acuteness, above all in that mysterious force of will which bends and warps more pliant natures to its own ends. Maxwell, watching him intently from the tree, could not but mark how scruple after scruple disappeared, how gradually and completely conviction seemed to steal over his countenance, as he followed step by step and argument by argument the bent of that master-mind which formed the third and dominant element in the conclave.

And who was this third conspirator, this evil spirit so much mightier and so much more daring than the two it controlled? Who but Moray, the Queen's half-brother. Staid, quiet, composed as usual; less splendidly dressed, less energetic in gesture, less striking in appearance than either of his companions, yet obviously the leader whom they trusted implicitly and obeyed without remorse.

One more faithful adherent to the House of Leslie completed the party. His honest face and loyal courage seemed strangely out of place where treason was brewing; a large handsome bloodhound kept close at the heel of Rothes, poking his wet nose at intervals into his master's hand.

Even in the extremity at which he found himself, Maxwell could not forbear contrasting the surrounding scene with the principal actors. The white stems of the beeches shone like silver in the glowing afternoon sun, while thrush and blackbird carolled gaily from the deep rich screen of their heavy foliage. Life and light, beauty and fragrance filled the atmosphere, peace and prosperity smiled around; white sheep were feeding on a grassy slope over against him between the trees; red roses blooming and clustering around steeped his senses in their perfumes; the bee hummed drowsily by in the warm still air; overhead the swallows flitted to and fro against the blue laughing sky: and there at his feet, within a spear's length of him, frowned the three dark pitiless faces, while Moray's measured voice unfolded the plot that chilled his very blood though it roused his vindictive hatred as he listened.

Not one of the others drank in every syllable as did that eager fugitive, crouching like a wild cat along the arm of the old beech tree.

'I tell ye, gentlemen, it cannot fail!' said the degenerate Stuart with more earnestness than usual;

'the net is so spread that fly which way she will the bird cannot but find herself within its meshes. I can tell ye for as certain as if I heard her say so now, that she leaves Perth after dinner to-morrow and rides to Callander, for the young Livingstone's baptism, direct; she will have no following beyond her personal attendants and some twenty or thirty spears. Your Leslies, my lord, may surely make account of these.'

He turned to Rothes while he spoke; the latter answered with a savage laugh, and the bloodhound murmured simultaneously a deep angry growl.

'Why, 'Hubert' seems to be of the same opinion,' pursued Moray, carelessly patting the dog's wide forehead, a liberty 'Hubert' seemed hugely inclined to resent. 'But I always counsel force enough in these little matters of necessity. "Never stretch your hand out farther than you can draw it back again," says our Scottish proverb; and "Never strike at your foe if your arm be not long enough to reach him," say those who know how to make war with prudence and moderation. Nay, I would have no risk run of failure or miscarriage for want of an odd score or two of horsemen. What say you, my lord of Argyle?'

That nobleman pondered a few moments ere he replied.

'My following moves forward to-night. I shall find four hundred spears at the Paren-Well to-morrow ere the sun has gone down two hours from the meridian.'

'Good!' answered Moray, nodding his head. 'And you, Rothes? The Leslies are sure to be swarming when there is aught stirring that promises a fight or a capture.'

'You shall count them yourself to-morrow, at sunrise, before we march,' answered the other gaily. 'If you drink a cup to-night, at supper, for every hundred men, your brain, my good Lord James, will hardly be so clear in the morning as you like to keep it when there is business to be done. Be quiet, 'Hubert!' the fiend's in the dog! What? down, man! art thou bewitched?'

The bloodhound's bristles were rising fiercer and fiercer, and he growled ominously as he snuffed the air with his broad black nostrils.

'Then this is the plan of the campaign,' resumed Moray. 'Argyle's forces and your own join at the Paren-Well, and in that lone district ye may dispose them to advantage, and keep the greater part out of sight from the Perth road. To avoid suspicion I would counsel that ye do not anticipate the hour of rendezvous. My imprudent sister might be informed even when some miles upon her journey, and turn back. When Her Grace's palfrey enters the pass at the Paren-Well, fourscore men-at-arms can do the business readily enough. If there is any attempt at resistance, another troop or two may strike in. Be careful to keep a large force fresh to protect Her Grace's sacred person when taken. I have arranged for her lodging to-morrow night with her kinswoman at Loch-Leven Castle. For the lady-faced lord, if not knocked o' the head in the skirmish, he must be disposed elsewhere. You shall have him at Leslie, Rothes, an' ye will, though I doubt you and Darnley are but unfriends at heart. We will meet in Edinburgh next week to consult on state affairs, but to-morrow, being Sabbath, I have thought well to explain my views to you both to-day. Gentlemen, I think we understand each other?'

Argyle murmured an assent. Rothes laughed again somewhat dangerously.

'If there is any resistance?' said he.

'I will not have a hair of Her Grace's head ruffled, or a fold of her dress,' replied Moray firmly. 'For the escort, they must be overpowered, of course; but Her Grace's person *shall* be respected, and her immediate attendants.'

'You promised me the Maries!' urged Rothes reproachfully; 'come, man, you shall not go back from your word; you promised me the whole four, or at least my pick of them. I would not have gone into it, but for the saucy Seton; and that sunny, silent lass, how call you her? Carmichael! I have ordered all sorts of toys to be here, expressly for them to-morrow. Down, 'Hubert!' be quiet, man!'

Maxwell's blood boiled within him, and he griped the branch of the beech as if it had been the last speaker's throat. Meantime 'Hubert' began baying furiously, glaring upwards into the tree with flaming eyes, and springing furiously against the trunk.

'The Maries must take their chance,' replied Moray, in the same quiet tones; 'if Her Grace be safe, I shall ask no questions. That dog hath cause for his uneasiness, my lord; take my word for it, we have been overheard. He scents a fresh foot in our neighbourhood.'

With a great oath Rothes drew his sword, and Argyle followed his example.

CHAPTER XXXVII.

' So soon. But now among all the rest
   The champion of a hero band,
With a gleaming blade and a flashing crest,
   And a haughty front and a ready hand.

' There cometh a crash, and a cry of need,
   A puff of smoke—and no more to tell,
But a dangling rein, and a plunging steed,
   And a rider lying where he fell.

' Ere the smoke hath melted in air above,
   Or the blood soaked in where the hoof hath trod,
The true heart beateth its last for its love,
   And the soul is gone home to God.'

HE moment was one of intense anxiety and terror. Concealed by the leaves of the old beech, every leap of the frantic bloodhound threatened to disclose the listener's hiding-place. The Earls of Rothes and Argyle, with drawn swords and bent brows, looked high and low for the cause of the dog's fury. Besides the dread of a violent death, all the more terrible at this his first hour of escape from captivity, Maxwell now felt that on him depended the liberty of his Queen; more than this, the life and honour of the woman he still so dearly loved.

To do him justice he would willingly have died on the spot to be able to advertise his Sovereign of her danger.

For an instant the desperate expedient darted through his mind of leaping down on Argyle's upturned face, wresting the sword from his grasp, and thus armed, doing battle with Moray and Rothes; but, even then, he reflected, how surely the former, who was never surprised or at a loss, would run to the Castle for assistance. If retaken, Walter shuddered to think, not of his own fate, but of Mary Carmichael's capture on the morrow.

Nevertheless there seemed nothing else for it; he had even collected his breath, and nerved his muscles for the spring, when a trumpet sounded in the Castle, and a puff of lurid smoke swept across the faces of the three noblemen, who were searching about with eager looks and bare blades, encouraging 'Hubert' the while with voice and gesture.

Again the smoke came rolling in a dun-coloured volume against the clear sky, and the bloodhound, his attention distracted by the new catastrophe, or his powers of scent dulled by the smell of fire, ceased to leap at the old tree, and lowering his stern, began to howl in abject terror and dismay.

Rothes could not forbear laughing, though he coughed and swore at the same time.

''Tis the alarm!' said he, as the trumpet again rang out in the castle-yard. 'Faith, Moray, I cannot but think they are burning the old house about our heads. Gentlemen both, I counted not to give ye so warm a reception as this!'

Nothing escaped Moray's quick eye. While they

hurried back towards the building, he observed the smoke and flames issuing from the turret Maxwell had so recently quitted.

'The wind is favourable,' said the Earl, as another cloud rolled over them, 'and you need not fear for more than the prison tower; for the sake of humanity, I trust, my lord, that it may be empty!'

Rothes did not answer; truth to say he had quite forgotten Walter Maxwell, and, even had he remembered him, would have thought the life of one poor prisoner mattered but little at such a time. The three noblemen addressed themselves to the task of quenching the fire with characteristic energy. Backed by the exertions of Rothes' disciplined followers, they soon succeeded in subduing the flames, and, ere night-fall, Leslie House had resumed its usual appearance of security, having suffered but little damage save the scorching of its outer wall. Poor old Ralph, however, was found dead in the dungeon, probably stifled by the smoke. But it is not with the inmates of Leslie that we have now to do.

As may be imagined, directly the coast was clear, Maxwell lost no time in slipping out of the tree. With a fervent thanksgiving in his heart, he dropped upon the sward, and ran as hard as his legs could carry him in the direction of the open country. Yet, even now, his situation was one of no ordinary hazard and embarrassment. He was unarmed; he was in an enemy's country; he might meet, at any moment, with retainers of Lord Rothes, who would recognize him at once for an escaped prisoner. Moreover, he was weaker than ordinary from his long confinement, and, even had it been otherwise, he could not expect to reach Perth on foot in time to warn the Queen of the plot laid against her person; and how was he to procure a horse? Cogitating these matters with considerable anxiety, he hurried on nevertheless, and was dismayed to find limbs and breath failing him as he ran.

To add to his discomfiture he heard footsteps approaching rapidly from behind. Turning his head, he espied the countryman whom he had already observed in the garden, nearing him with every stride.

Maxwell would have given ten years of his life ungrudgingly to have had as many inches of steel in his belt.

"'Od sake, man, ye can run as weel as fight!' exclaimed a familiar voice close to him, as the fugitive slackened speed to collect his strength for the desperate struggle he anticipated. 'Keep wast, hinny! keep wast! down yon burnie-side. I can hear 'Wanton Willie' nickerin' at us the noo!'

Though they still kept on at a rapid pace, between running and walking, Maxwell's hand was fast locked in that of 'Dick-o'-the-Cleugh,' whilst the borderer, pointing to a neighbouring brake in which a confederate, with two led horses, was concealed, in a tone of suppressed triumph, assured his friend that he was safe.

It took but little time to mount 'Wanton Willie,' the redoubtable bay that Dick affirmed was the pride of his lord's stable, and less to inform the borderer of the plot against Her Majesty, and the necessity for reaching Perth with the utmost speed they could command. As they swung along at a hand-gallop, Dick, with many a smothered laugh and quaint allusion, for he looked on the whole performance, from first to last, as an unparalleled jest, detailed to his companion the measures he had adopted to effect his delivery.

Translated from his own vernacular, the borderer's account was as follows:

After his interview with the Queen and her ladies, in Edinburgh, he had ridden on to Leslie with the intention of rescuing Walter with the strong hand; but on arriving in Fife he found that country in so alarmed a state, and Leslie House itself so securely watched and strongly garrisoned, that such a project was utterly impracticable. His predatory habits had taught Dick, long ago, that where force was useless, resort must be had to stratagem, and he set about his task with all the quiet energy of his character, and the craft of his profession.

In the first place it was necessary to diminish his retinue, in order to avoid suspicion. 'Lang Willie' and 'Jock-o'-the-Hope' accordingly were despatched back to Hermitage, leaving one of their horses for the use of the prisoner, and Ralph Armstrong, a sedate and cautious old jack-man, remained at a considerable distance from Leslie, with the three horses, which he kept well exercised, and fit for a trial of speed and endurance at any moment.

Dick then, disguising himself like a countryman, applied for a day's work or two in the gardens and pleasure-grounds of Leslie, and ere long his great strength and inexhaustible good-humour so won upon the gardener, that he was installed as a regular labourer about the place.

Here he soon made himself acquainted with the passages and entrances of the stronghold, more especially with the geography of the dungeon-tower. Nevertheless, study it as he would, he could find no means of communicating with the captive, much less of liberating him from thraldom. A thick iron door between massive stone walls is no ineffectual barrier, if only it be kept locked.

Turning matters over and over in his own mind, while he worked away in the flower-garden, Dick had arrived at the conclusion that the shortest method would be to set the whole place on fire, seize his keys, after braining old Ralph the gaoler in the confusion, and thus make his escape with the prisoner through the flames. To his great relief he had long since ascertained, amidst the gossip of the servants, that Maxwell was still alive.

It was necessary, however, to choose a judicious moment for this exploit, and Dick, understanding that the Lord Rothes and a large force were to move on the Sabbath from Leslie, had selected that day, when the house would be less strictly guarded than usual, for his undertaking. His plan was to fire the place about the hour of curfew, when the retainers were sauntering abroad in the summer evening, and were less easily collected than at any other hour; but as our borderer was a man of great rapidity in action, and kept himself ready at any moment to take an advantage, Armstrong had strict directions whenever, by day or night, he should see a wreath of smoke or a red glare above the old beeches, that instant the horses should be brought to a certain secluded coppice within half a mile of the Castle.

Thus our friend laid his plans, and with equal judgment disposed his combustibles, straw by straw, as it were, and faggot by faggot, even as the bird of the air builds her nest, with secrecy and perseverance. Everything was ready, and the borderer went about his work in the garden, as he said himself, 'with a clear conscience.' On this very afternoon, when Maxwell made his unaided escape from confinement, Dick had just returned from attending the three noblemen to their game at bowls—the very game which Maxwell had remarked unfinished as he crossed the green. It was with no small surprise that he saw the prisoner escaping across the garden which was his own peculiar charge.

The borderer was somewhat disconcerted; nevertheless he reflected for a moment: 'If,' thought he, 'Mr. Maxwell can surmount the outer wall he will but light down plump amongst the three Earls who are walking in the avenue beyond; if he remain concealed here in the garden, he is sure to be missed when old Ralph visits the prison, discovered, and retaken; nay, if Rothes be the least out of humour, probably put to death. The faggots are all laid; I have a flint and steel in my belt; I had best set fire to the place at once, and have done with it.'

Moreover, Dick was not very sure on his own account that he might not be himself suspected. In getting the bowls ready for the three noblemen, Moray's piercing glance had not failed to detect a face he seemed to recognize. With a brief effort of memory the Earl recalled that thrust on the causeway of Edinburgh from mad Arran's blade, and the interposition of Earl Bothwell's henchman, which saved his own life.

'Good fellow,' said he, as Dick raised his face from setting 'the jack' in its place, 'I have seen you before; I owe you a debt for saving my life a while ago, during a brawl in the High-street.'

Argyle and Rothes were at the other end of the green, poising their bowls to begin; Dick answered hastily, and in a whisper,

'I've been in trouble on the Border; I'm in trouble yet; but I'm no kent in Fife. Your honour can best pay it by no lettin' on* that ye've ever seen me before!'

Moray was a good-natured man enough; he nodded an understanding, and put a piece of gold in the gardener's hand; but, nevertheless, Dick felt none the more sanguine, after this recognition, for the success of his enterprise.

No sooner however had he seen Maxwell swing himself into the old beech tree, a gymnastic feat which called forth his warmest approval, than he hastened back to put his long laid scheme in practice, with what success we have already learned, for the bloodhound's sagacity must unquestionably have led to a discovery of the fugitive, had it not been for the diversion occasioned by the fire.

'An' noo,' said the borderer, with a sad wistful expression on his honest face, very different from the roguish humour with which he had narrated the detail of his adventure; 'an' noo, I'm easy in my mind, whichever way the bowl may rin. I've paid my debt, maister Maxwell, ye ken; I'm thinking it'll no be lang or I get my quittance.'

---

* 'Lettin' on'— Scottice for disclosing a secret.

Maxwell was somewhat puzzled; he could not quite fathom the meaning of his honest friend. Alas! ere a few hours were past he understood it but too well.

Time of course was the chief object with the three cavaliers; it was indispensable to arrive in Perth at as early an hour as possible, so as to warn the Queen of her danger, and to raise the country for the punishment of her foes. The party however were right well mounted; Dick had not selected the *worst* of Bothwell's horses for an expedition in which speed was so likely to be an essential element of success; and 'Wanton Willie,' once the property of Lord Scrope himself, and stolen from the English Warden by a series of stratagems, remarkable alike for ingenuity and audacity, was an animal of extraordinary power, mettle, and endurance.

It was no ordinary sensation of delight that Maxwell experienced as he swept through the evening air borne onwards by the long untiring stride of the powerful bay stallion. It was like grasping the hand of an old friend to stroke and smooth that swelling crest as 'Wanton Willie' tossed his head and snorted, champing the bit and snatching playfully at the rein.

He had always loved a good horse well. Now with the fate of a kingdom dependent on its speed, he could not prize too highly the merits of his charger. Also Maxwell's heart was even yet sore and empty; it was soothing to rely on the honest fidelity of a brute. How many men are there who lavish on horse and hound the affections that were hoarded, it may be long ago, elsewhere; given unreservedly, accepted with glee, and returned after awhile to the dejected owner with the sap dried up, the core extracted, and the virtue gone. So he learns to content himself perforce with that which is real and substantial, at least as far as it goes; learns to thrill at the note of a hound, forget the past in the glowing excitement of a gallop; and the well-judging world opines that he has a grovelling soul which soars not above the stables and the kennel, and is fit for no better things.

The moon was coming up from the horizon, and still the three rode swiftly and steadily on. They were many miles from Leslie now, but, alas! they were not yet clear of Leslie's influence. At a small hamlet where they stopped to water and refresh their horses, Maxwell was recognized ere he touched the ground by a scion of the House of Rothes, even then on the march with a party of horse to join his kinsman's forces at the Paren-Well.

David Leslie started with surprise as the bay was pulled up at the stone trough before the village inn, but the young soldier was prompt in action and saw at a glance he had but three men to deal with, and one of those unarmed. His own retainers were numerous and on the spot.

'Walter Maxwell!' he exclaimed, seizing 'Wanton Willie,' at the same instant by the bridle, 'you are my prisoner! Ho! a Leslie! a Leslie! to the rescue!'

His men came pouring out at the well-known cry. Stout troopers all of them, and armed besides to the teeth. There was nothing for it but a quick and determined resistance.

Dick spurred his horse without hesitation against the assailant on foot, dealing him at the same moment a heavy buffet with his gauntleted hand, for he had no time to draw his sword. Armstrong protected Maxwell's other flank. There were several fierce oaths, a pistol-shot, a smothered groan, much trampling of hoofs, a plunge or two, and Maxwell found himself again careering along between his two defenders over the open plain at a pace that set pursuit at defiance.

'Well out of that, Dick!' said he cheerily, as they pulled their horses at last into a trot, and listened for the enemy who came not. 'Well out of that! we'll win the race and be home now before midnight, I expect. These are rare stuff, these Border nags of yours; it's no wonder men should be tempted to steal such cattle as we are riding to-night!'

But Dick answered nothing, only he seemed to hold his horse in a rigid immovable grasp, and the three broke into a gallop even swifter than before.

The moon was up now riding clear and high in the mid-heaven. Was it only her light that made the borderer's face so pale?

Dick spoke at last in a thick hoarse voice, and the others pulled up simultaneously as he did so.

'I'll light doun, I'm thinkin',' said he. 'Ride *you* on, maister Maxwell! I'll just bide where I am awee. It's a kin' o' dwam*-like that's come over me.'

He dismounted while he spoke. He was scarce clear of the saddle ere he staggered and fell heavily to the ground. Armstrong unbuckled his corslet and opened the buff jerkin beneath. It was light enough for Maxwell to see the little round mark that soldiers know so well.

---

* Dwam—a swoon.

Large drops were standing on the borderer's forehead, and his lips were turning white. Maxwell took his hand, and the dying man smiled a feeble, ghastly smile as he returned the grasp.

'I'll no win back to Liddesdale,' said he faintly. 'I'll no get the length o' Perth the night. I'll be meat for the corbies* the morn. Gude speed ye, my canny lad! Pit yer foot intill the stirrup again. A Queen's errans munna stan' still for the like o' me!'

Maxwell's tears fell thick and fast. While Armstrong held the horses, he propped the borderer's head upon his knee, and whispered a few broken words, he knew not what, of grief and hope, that seemed a mockery even then.

The mossy turf on which they rested was not more clammy than the pale forehead in its damps of death; he was bleeding inwardly, and every breath he drew exhausted more and more the shallow stream of vitality that was left.

'Ride *you* on,' he whispered, 'ride *you* on! leave Ralph wi' *me*; I'll no keep him lang. Ye'll win to the Court the morn, lad, an' ye'll see bonny mistress Seton, an' ye'll tell her frae me ——'

He was getting very weak now; twice or thrice he strove to speak, but no sound came. Maxwell bent over him, and held his breath to catch the sacred accents of the dying man.

He raised himself a little with an effort, and his voice was stronger now.

'Tell her,' said he, 'that if ever she can win to

---

* Corbies—crows.

Liddesdale, she maun walk afoot through the bonny glens, and hearken to the lilt o' the lavrock, an' pu' a sprig o' the red heather, just to mind her o' 'Dick-o'-the-Cleugh'—rough, rantin' Dick, that wadna ha' evened himself to kiss the very ground beneath her feet. Eh! lad, an' she hadna been a born leddy, I wad hae lo'ed you lassie weel!'

Then Dick's head sank lower and lower; nor, although he lived for a short space afterwards, was he heard to speak again.

Maxwell was forced to leave him, however loth, in charge of his comrade; his own duty would admit of no delay. Sadly and slowly he mounted 'Wanton Willie' once more; sadly and slowly he loitered away at a foot's-pace, turning his head often to gaze wistfully back where Ralph Armstrong was stooping in the moonlight over the long prostrate figure of the henchman. At last he saw Ralph lay the head gently down upon the sward, and walk a few paces away. Then he knew that it was over, and galloped on towards Perth with wet eyes and a heavy heart.

CHAPTER XXXVIII.

'For though her smiles were sad and faint,
   And though her voice was low,
She never murmured a complaint,
   Nor hinted at her woe,
Nor harboured in her gentle breast
   The lightest thought of ill;
Giving all, forgiving all,
   Pure and perfect still.

'Confiding when the world was hard,
   And kind when it was cold,
What wealth of Love was stored and barred
   Within that Heart of Gold!
Exulting every grief to share,
   And every task fulfil;
Giving all, forgiving all,
   Fond and faithful still.

'And when upon that patient brow
   The storm had broke at last,
And all her pride was shattered now,
   And all her power was past,
She meekly kissed the hand that smote,
   And yielded to its will;
Giving all, forgiving all,
   True and tender still.'

APPY'S the wooing that's not long of doing,' says a hopeful Scottish proverb. 'Marry in haste, and repent at leisure,' is a wholesome English warning, that may be considered the converse of the above.

'Some, by construction, deem these words misplaced,
 At leisure marry, and repent in haste,'

quoth Congreve, or one of the old dramatists. We may take our choice of maxims on the important topic of wedlock, satisfied that, ponder on it as we may, it is a matter in which blind fortune concerns herself more than in any other of our human affairs. Yes, ' your marriage goes by destiny,' no doubt, and sometimes the Fates draw you off nectar, and sometimes wholesome bitters, and sometimes weak, insipid, flat and stale small beer. Under any circumstances it is better not to pull a wry face at the draught. If the fairest woman the earth ever saw could not make sure of conjugal happiness, who has a right to complain?

Darnley was now Duke of Albany—the handsomest duke in Christendom—and on the evening before her nuptials his affianced bride had somewhat prematurely caused him to be proclaimed King of Scotland. Two religions had prepared to consecrate the tie; the Pope's dispensation, inasmuch as the lovers were blood relations, had been obtained from Rome, and the banns by which, according to the Reformed Persuasion, ' Harry Duke of Albany and Earl of Ross should be united to Mary, by the grace of God, Queen of Scots, and Sovereign of the Realm,' had been proclaimed in the parish church of the Canongate.

The Queen had escaped the plot laid against her by her enemies, at Leslie House, and, it is needless to say, how royal favour and ladies' smiles were showered upon the daring rider, who foundered ' Wanton Willie ' for ever by the speed with which he brought his timely intelligence to Perth, a speed that enabled the Queen to sweep down to her capital with a strong, well-mounted escort, in advance of all the preparations made for her capture. She had quelled an insurrection at St. Leonard's Craigs since then; she had strengthened her party by all the means at her disposal, and even striven hard to listen without anger to the ill-timed remonstrances of Elizabeth, forwarded through Randolph, who, somewhat to his dismay, and much to his disgust, found his importance waning, hour by hour, at the Scottish Court.

Everything a woman *could* do by persuasion, by policy, by forbearance, by her own intrinsic fascination, Mary had done to attain, if possible, a few months or even weeks of repose for the enjoyment of the present; happy, as she fancied herself, in her love, and willing to be at peace with all the world.

And while the young Queen looked about her for friends and partisans in every direction, was it likely that she would forget her stout champion on the Border, the warlike Earl of Bothwell? It may be that she had long sought an excuse to pardon him; it may be that like the rest of her sex, though prone to commit it in haste, her heart smote her sore, after a while, for an act of injustice. She re-called him, she forgave him, she brought him back to her dangerous presence, and the flame that was consuming this wild and tameless heart, only burned all the fiercer that he must stifle it for a while.

Moray kept aloof from the sister whom he had deceived and the Queen against whom he had conspired. Accustomed as Mary had been for so long to depend upon her brother whenever she needed counsel or assistance, no doubt she felt his estrangement very keenly; but even Moray, notwithstanding all his offences, she would have received once more with open arms, had he abjured his devotion to the interests of the astute Elizabeth, and returned to his natural duty and allegiance.

The fairest daughter of the Stuarts was always, alas! more of the woman than the Queen. Had she been less frank, less trusting, less kindly, less affectionate, above all, less beautiful, the crown of Scotland would have sat more firm upon her head, the head itself would not at last have been severed by the cruel axe at Fotheringay.

But that dainty head never looked more nobly than to-day. With the glory of love and happiness shining round it; with the royal diadem resting on the white and gentle brow; with the soft rich hair gathered into such a coronet of splendour as no other princess, as no other *woman* in Europe could boast; with a majestic form set off by the sweeping robes of *black* in which, as a royal widow, etiquette bade her approach the altar; above all with the atmosphere of beauty that surrounded Mary as with a charm, old Thomas the Rhymer had never such a vision of the Fairy Queen herself, as burst upon the sight of loyal Lennox and devoted Athol, when she emerged from her chamber and suffered them to conduct her to the Chapel-Royal of Holyrood, at six of the clock on the summer Sabbath morning that smiled with such well-omened brilliancy upon the bride.

Could black Fate be hovering over that gay and sparkling throng, marking them out, as it were, one by one, for her future shafts? There they stood—so many of them; the brave, the beautiful, the loyal, the gentle, and the true, glowing in youth and health, towering in the prime of manhood and the pride of place; radiant in silks and velvets, blazing with gold and gems; and the red mark scored in the book of destiny against two out of every three illustrious names, and the little cloud, though still below the horizon, yet waiting none the less surely to break in fatal tempest over the proud unconscious brows, and shatter the guilty and the innocent in one indiscriminate ruin to the dust.

Even crook-backed Riccio could not forbear an exultant song of rejoicing when the ceremony was concluded, that gave his indulgent Mistress to the handsome petulant boy she had chosen for her lord.

'Glory to God,' exclaimed the Secretary, in his deep rich tones as the rites were finished with a burst of chanted thanksgiving. How long was it ere those same lips, writhing in their death-pang, were gasping for mercy in hoarse gurgling whispers choked in blood? In the meantime, the Queen is conducted back from the Chapel to the Palace, and the ceremony takes place of unrobing Her Majesty, who is now no longer a widow, but a bride, with all the established jests and noisy glee such an occasion is calculated to call forth.

First Darnley takes out a pin, then Athol, then Lennox, then each of the gentlemen of the household as he can approach the royal person, while her ladies, like a guard of Amazons close round her more and more as the spoliation proceeds. The process, as is natural, soon degenerates into something like a romp, and Walter Maxwell, with a heavy heart, finds himself, to his own dismay, mixed up with such merry fooleries.

While Her Majesty proceeds with a few of her tiring-women into another chamber, whence she will presently re-appear in dazzling apparel suited to the occasion, we will return to the humbler personages of the scene, who may now, like the supernumeraries in a theatre, come up to the footlights and display their antics, whilst their betters are off the stage.

To begin with the Maries, whom we have too much neglected whilst taken up with ruder and less engaging natures.

Those young ladies, by the very act to which they have even now been lending their assistance, have become freed from their self-imposed obligations of celibacy, and might marry, if it so pleased them, one and all to-morrow. To the philosopher who fancies he understands the nature of the sex, it will not appear surprising that at this juncture none of them should show the slightest disposition for entering that holy state, from which it has hitherto been considered such an extreme hardship they should be debarred. Hilarious, as it was their duty to appear during the performance of Her Majesty's nuptials; hilarious, of course be it understood, with the proper admixture of tears, for ladies esteem a wedding to be essentially an April performance of showers and sunshine; yet no sooner was the principal excitement over, no sooner were the four young beauties released from their respective attitudes of attention, and at liberty to receive the compliments and reply to the bantering congratulations of the courtiers, than a cloud seemed to come over each of them, and they looked far less inclined to laugh than to cry.

Mary Beton, perhaps, kept her spirits up with more determination and a greater show of indifference than either of her sisters in sorrow; nevertheless, Mary Beton, while she certainly enjoyed an advantage over the others, was in an uncomfortable state of uncertainty and transition.

Although it is doubtless a wise and wholesome precaution for a lady to have two strings to her bow, yet the instrument is apt to get somewhat warped and out of order in the process of taking off the old and fitting on the new. There is something softening as well as soothing in the attentions of the recent capture, and they remind us rather touchingly at times of those other looks and tones which made such fools of us not so long ago. We cannot do the same things, say the same words, go through the same exercises, (and in truth, there is, we believe, but little variety in the drill by which the human heart is disciplined,) without experiencing very much the same kind of sensations as heretofore, and it is not always easy to distinguish between the old feelings and the new. The former come over us with an overwhelming rush when we least expect them, and our only chance is to credit the fresh account with as much of the balance as we can. That same tenant-right is a very difficult matter to get rid of when once it has been firmly established in the breast.

Mary Beton had broke with her old lover for good and all. She had convicted him of treason to her Queen; and although this offence she might possibly have forgiven, she had found him out in treachery to herself. It is needless to say that she would have nothing more to do with Randolph, and was prepared to listen with no unwilling ear to the suit of Alexander Ogilvy. But the latter was distant and offended still. He had not forgotten certain rebuffs, certain black looks and cold answers that had piqued and irritated him long ago. He loved her indeed very dearly, therefore he did not mean to hold out for any great length of time, but still, it was *his* turn now, and he could not be expected to forego his share of advantage in the merciless game. It is an old saying that 'many a heart is caught on the rebound,' and perhaps he was sure of his prey, and content to wait a little and enjoy the excitement of the capture.

Proud mistress Beton, too, had become far more docile and womanly of late. Pained and humbled by the treatment she had experienced from Randolph, it would have been inexpressibly soothing and delightful to encourage and return an attachment she could trust, and on which she could lean, so to speak, without fear of mortification. Great liberties are sometimes taken, great risks run, in these affairs. Tempers that are imperturbable on all other topics, blaze up with reckless violence against the nearest and dearest. When the wild bird has ruffled her plumes in anger and broken her jesses in pique, the observant fowler, who watches his opportunity, finds every facility afforded for his lure. There is no time at which the human heart is so susceptible to kindness as when writhing under a sense of injustice and ill-treatment which it has not deserved.

So Mary Beton was less haughty, less overbearing, and, consequently, looked ten times lovelier than usual on her Mistress's wedding day.

She stands now nearest the door, waiting for the Queen, and whispers gently and lovingly to Mary Seton, who seems to cling to her senior as to an elder sister, and whose fair face has of late assumed a sad and thoughtful expression very different from that which it used to wear.

The arch looks are downcast now, and the merry voice is hushed and low. The girl is not unhappy, only grave and saddened perhaps a little by her experiences. She has bid Walter tell her over and over again how poor Dick Rutherford laid him down to die in the moonlight and spoke of her—of *her*, the vain frivolous girl!—with the last breath he ever drew. What had she done to win so entirely the devotion of that great honest heart? Had she suspected it? Had she triumphed in it? Had she prized it? Ah! never so much as now, when all the wishing in the world would fail to bring the trusting kindly nature back to her feet.

She was a noble damsel, and Dick but the mere retainer of a warlike lord, ranking scarce above a man-at-arms. And yet it was something, surely, to have been so loved by any one human heart: to have taken everything and given nothing in return. She could weep now to think that never—never would she be able to make him amends.

Aye, he was a *man* that was; brave and strong and single-minded, daring, patient, resolute, fearing nothing under Heaven, humble and child-like only with *her.* How often might she unwittingly have wrung the gentle uncomplaining heart; how often purposely, just to essay and feel her power. She could hate herself to think of a hundred trifles now. Ah! too late —too late! He was gone where neither foeman's lance nor lady's look could reach; where cold words and bare steel were alike powerless to wound. Gone—gone altogether, and she would *never* see him more.

It seemed to Mary Seton, as she stood there and looked at her comrades, that she alone would fulfil that vow of celibacy from which to-day's festival had enfranchised the Queen's Maries. Where could she expect to find hereafter such an affection as she had neglected and lost? No; henceforth she would devote herself heart and hand to the service of her Mistress; cling to the Queen through rain and shine, calm and storm, good and evil. If prosperity blessed her dear Mistress she would rejoice; if adversity frowned, she would console her; if danger or calamity came, she would share it. Let the others marry, an' they must; for her, she would belong to her Queen! And nobly, in after years, Mary Seton redeemed her vow.

But there was one of the maids-of-honour whose wedding was, indeed, to succeed Her Majesty's, who looked forward to its arrival with more than maidenly longing; who hoped for it, and relied on it with more than a woman's trust. Mary Hamilton, with her pale face and wasted form, had continued her service with the Queen, silent and uncomplaining, never unbosoming herself to her companions, not even confiding her sorrows to her Mistress, until now. To-morrow she would be free; to-morrow would be the day of her espousals, and the poor weary head would lay itself to rest, the poor sore heart find comfort and relief at last. It was for this she had been waiting so patiently, for this she had borne her burden so uncomplainingly. To-morrow she would become the Bride of Heaven, and the veil she would then put on must never be taken off again this side the grave!

In her cell (so her religion taught her, hopeful even in death), in her cell she could pray for the soul of him she had loved so fondly; could believe, when his fiery sufferings and her own prayers and tears had obliterated his crimes, she would meet him, never again to part, on the shining hills beyond the dark shadowy valley that she feared no whit, nay, that she only longed to tread.

Mary Hamilton took the vows on the day subsequent to the Queen's marriage, at the bright midsummer season, when the blooming world should have looked fairest and most captivating to her who turned her back upon it so willingly for evermore. During a twelvemonth, so the Romish Church enforced, she must make trial of her new profession, and at the expiration of that period, should she continue in the same mind, the novice was to become a nun.

There is little doubt she would have fulfilled her intention had the occasion ever arrived.

It was an early harvest that year in Scotland, but ere the barley was white, Mary Hamilton had done with nuns and nunneries, vows and ceremonies, withered hopes and mortal sorrows, and had gone to that place where the weary heart can alone find the rest it has so longed for at last.

There is but one more of the Maries with whom we have to do: mistress Carmichael must speak for herself in another chapter.

CHAPTER XXXIX.

'For love will wear through shine and shower,
  And love can bear to bide its time;
Unwearied at the vesper-hour,
  As when the matins chime.

'And love can strive against a host,
  Can watch and wait and suffer long;
Still daring more when fearing most,
  In very weakness strong.

'Though bruised and sore, it never dies,
  Though faint and weary, standing fast;
It never fails, and thus the prize
  Is won by *love* at last.'

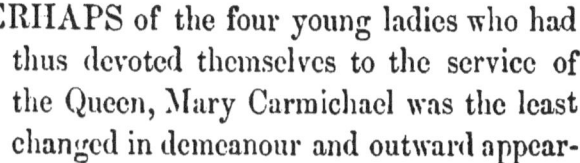ERHAPS of the four young ladies who had thus devoted themselves to the service of the Queen, Mary Carmichael was the least changed in demeanour and outward appearance at the auspicious period which gave them their freedom, and entitled them to assume that temporary dominion over the other sex which is a woman's birthright. She was still beautiful as ever; her sorrows, if she had any, did not veil an atom of brilliancy in her eye, or take a shade of colour from her cheek; her figure was no less rounded and symmetrical in its full flowing lines, her step no less firm and haughty, her

manner, if anything, colder and more self-reliant. If there was any change observable in Mary Carmichael, it was that she seemed to become harder, prouder, less sympathizing and less womanly day by day.

On some natures anxiety and distress produce a bracing, and as it were a petrifying effect; they will not have it thought that they can be affected by such morbid influences as the feelings. There are women of ice and women of fire, women of wax and women of marble. It is possible that if the truth were known, these strong beauties suffer as much as their more impressionable sisters, and yet the proud face never falls, the hard eyes never soften; try her with words that ought to stab, each of them, to the quick, if she winces you never know it, for the white bosom heaves no higher, the colour neither fades nor deepens on the fair provoking cheek. It is maddening to the assailant; perhaps also the one attacked is not quite so comfortable as she looks; perhaps if you were to alter your tactics, to change your mood and take up the cool indifferent line yourself, she might be goaded out of this unnatural calm into a tempest, that if it did break out would probably be very terrible. It is better not to try. 'Touch not the cat but a glove,' says the motto of a noble Scottish family; 'Never drive a woman into a corner' is the maxim of every philosopher who would escape scathless from those contests in which the rougher and honester nature is almost sure to come by the worst.

Walter Maxwell was not the man to persevere in a wooing that he once had reason to believe was unwelcome; he, too, could hide a warm loving heart under a grave impenetrable brow—could bear the pain of seeing the idol of his fancy day by day more and more estranged, yet never wince nor writhe under the torture, far less upbraid or complain. For weeks he had been habitually in her society, himself the hero of the hour, the man whom the Queen favoured as her deliverer, whom lords and ladies greeted as her champion, yet never hazarded a word nor look that could lead Mary Carmichael to believe he still cared for her, far less sought an interview, as doubtless she often hoped he would, that should bring about reproaches, tears, a quarrel, an explanation, and a reconciliation.

These two proud dispositions were like the parallel lines, which, similar in all their properties, are for that reason incapable of meeting. How the woman's heart swelled and ached when she watched him always so calm, so courteous, so impassable, so indifferent; how she longed for him to be rude, fierce, angry, even unjust and unreasonable; she would rather he had *struck* her than thus passed her by with that studiously gentle manner, that hateful iron smile. Oh! it was hard to bear—hard to bear, and yet she *must* bear it, and none must know her weakness or her sufferings.

And he, too, longing only to forgive everything in which he felt himself aggrieved, believing he could be quite content now if they were but *friends* and nothing more, thirsting for one kind look from her eyes, one cordial word from her lips, felt bound perforce to treat her with the calm, courteous, defiant bearing of those who are enemies to the death.

Ludicrous as it might have been to the bystanders, it was an uncomfortable state of things to the per-

formers themselves in the little drama,—tragedy,
comedy, farce, call it what you will, and your nomen-
clature will probably depend upon your time of life.
Lovers' quarrels look so different as the decades roll
by. An uncomfortable state of things, doubtless, and
it might have gone on for a life-time but for one of
those accidents to which such sufferers are peculiarly
susceptible.

Accidents, like the fresh breeze that springs up
on a sultry summer's day. The heavens are dark and
lowering, there is an oppressive weight in the atmosphere, the very birds sit hushed and sullen behind
the motionless leaves, and the earth looks saddened
and weary, mourning as if she had made up her mind
that the sun was never to shine again. Suddenly the
breeze wakes up and comes laughing out of the west;
the clouds fly scattered before him, the young leaves
flicker in the golden sunshine, the birds burst forth
in those joyous strains which, to do them justice, they
are ever ready to strike up on the slightest provocation, and the whole landscape shines and smiles and
quivers in life and light once more.

When the Queen emerged from her tiring-room in
the magnificent apparel best befitting such a bride,
another courtier, in addition to the party that had
thronged the Chapel, entered the royal circle to tender
his homage as in duty bound, and congratulate Her
Majesty on her nuptials.

This new arrival was a tall handsome man of middle
age, perhaps a little past that elusive epoch, yet still
bearing the traces of considerable beauty of feature,
and distinguished for peculiar fascination of manner

and grace of bearing. He was dressed, too, with the utmost splendour, and obviously in the very latest fashion of the French Court. Several of the Queen's immediate attendants seemed to know him well, and greeted him with a warm assumption of cordiality and interest, although in the outer circle, so to speak, enquiring glances were shot at the welcome stranger, and whispers of 'Who is he? who is he?' passed unanswered from mouth to mouth.

It was chiefly among the younger courtiers and those whose rank did not entitle them to share the secret counsels of Her Majesty, that this curiosity was observed to manifest itself. Two or three of the seniors accosted him with obviously suppressed warmth and mirthful looks that denoted a world of intelligence only known to themselves, but Mary Carmichael's eyes rested on the distinguished stranger with an expression of the utmost love and confidence those very expressive eyes could convey.

Had it not been for this, Maxwell might never have remarked the late addition to the royal circle, so absent was he and pre-occupied, truth to say, so utterly weary and sick at heart. Watching, however, as he had accustomed himself to do, by stealth, the direction of his mistress's glances, he could not but be aware of the stranger's presence, and it needed no second look to satisfy him that this was the identical cavalier whom he had seen that starlight night in the Abbey-garden, whose face and figure he was not likely to forget should he live for a hundred years. On that memorable occasion, he remembered to have experienced a vague and puzzling sensation that he had met his rival before. To-day, in the Queen's presence-chamber, it came back again; but he was in no mood now to speculate on such random fancies and probabilities.

No, in five seconds of time he had made up his mind to the worst, and had resolved upon the line of conduct he should adopt.

Of course it was all over at last. Never till this moment, when it crumbled and fell to ashes, had he been aware how much of hope there was mingled with his suspicions and his pique. Hope! the word itself seemed an absurdity now. Nevertheless, there is no such utter composure as a brave mind borrows from the total annihilation of all it has loved and cherished most. Men *can* have no anxieties when there is nothing left to lose, and even a coward will sometimes die gracefully enough if there be an obvious impossibility of escape.

The most accomplished gallant of the French Court could not have moved through the circle of ladies that crowded the Queen's ante-room with a more assured air than did Walter Maxwell; the most consummate fop could not have shown less agitation than was betrayed in the few words he addressed then and there to mistress Carmichael.

'We were old friends once,' said he, 'though now we seldom even speak. Shall I find you in the gallery before the banquet? I should like to be friends again once for all.'

He might have been criticising the pattern of her dress, so cold and quiet were his tones. The lady did not show quite so much self-command. She turned very pale, and her lip trembled so that she did not dare trust her voice; but she bowed her head in the affirmative, and was glad to screen herself from observation meanwhile amongst the ample dresses of her companions.

You see she had by no means made up her mind that all *was* over; perhaps too, a horrible misgiving came across her that she might have driven him too far.

While the rest of the household were preparing for the banquet, they had the gallery to themselves. Strange to say, the lady reached the trysting-place first. Though the colour deepened on her cheek when she heard his step, she never turned her head till he came close to her, and by that time she had recovered her self-command. They were standing on the very spot where she had dropped the roses long ago. If this coincidence occurred to her, be sure she did not think it worth while to mention it.

He spoke first, very gravely and kindly, in the tone of a man who feels he has a reparation to make.

'Mistress Carmichael,' said he, 'I have treated you unfairly and unlike a friend. I may have thought I had a right to be angry with you; now I know for certain that is all over. I am no longer angry. I ask you to forgive me, and to shake hands before we part.'

She scarcely dared look at him, standing there tall and manly before her, with his kind eyes, and bold, frank brow. No fopling lover to be given up lightly and at a moment's notice, forsooth! Over, was it? Perhaps she did not see it at all in that light!

'What do you mean?' she gasped, trying hard not to tremble, nor to laugh, nor indeed to cry.

'I am reconciled to it all,' was his answer, 'because I see you love him, and that you are happy. It is but a selfish affection that cannot rejoice in the welfare of its object. To-day,' he added, with rather a sad smile, 'the maiden's vow is at an end. Never mind what follies may have once crossed my brain. Prove to me that you forgive them by confiding in me as if I was your brother.'

She looked up at him with a quick searching glance.

'You mean you think I am going to be married?' said she, 'and you are wishing me joy?'

'I am indeed,' he replied, with another smile yet sadder than the last. 'Somewhat awkwardly, I fear, yet none the less honestly for that. Listen. I shall never tell you so again. I loved you as dearly as it is possible for man to love woman; so dearly that even now I can rejoice that you are happy. I can give you up to one you love. I can ask you now at this moment, when everything is at an end between us except friendship, the purest and most loyal, to let me serve you all my life; though it will be years before I shall have courage to look on your face again.'

The last sentence came out in spite of him. It spoke volumes to a woman's perceptions. Perhaps she liked that involuntary confession of weakness better than all the strength and self-denial she had so admired awhile ago.

'You do *really* love me,' said she, trembling indeed still, but pale no longer, 'so well, that for my happiness you would give up everything, even myself?'

'Had it not been so,' he answered, 'do you think I should have been so angry with you for what I saw in the Abbey-garden? Well, he may claim you now before them all. God bless you and *him!* Farewell! Will you not give me your hand once more for the last time?'

She must have been a strangely unfeeling lady, mistress Mary Carmichael, to resist such an appeal, and yet the tears were brimming in her eyes despite of a roguish happy smile on her red lips. She withheld her hand, however. Perhaps she did not wish to part quite so abruptly.

'You are generous,' said she, between tears and laughter, 'and you used to be obedient—at least sometimes. Wilful always, you know, or I should not have had to chide you so often. Will you shake my—my future husband by the hand, and assure him of your good will?'

He thought she might have spared him this, but he assented cordially. What mattered it, a little suffering more or less? At least it would put off the parting for a few minutes.

'Wait here an instant while I bring him!' said she, and darted off leaving Walter in that frame of mind which is best described by the metaphor of 'not knowing whether he stood on his head or his heels.'

He had not long to wait, though in truth he kept no account of time. A light hurrying footstep trod the gallery once more, followed by a heavier and manlier stride. Maxwell turned round to confront his lost love, closely followed by the individual she had promised to bring.

'Tis strange how a vague misty idea that has puzzled us for long, will sometimes shine out on a sudden as clear as day. There was a frank, joyous expression on the stranger's brow, a sparkle of excitement in his eye, that brought back to Maxwell's recollection for the first time where he had seen him before the well-remembered night in the Abbey-garden. It was the same tall cavalier who had spurred his horse so gallantly into the skirmish near Hermitage, shouting his war-cry the while. It was a kinsman, then, whom she was going to marry after all.

Mary Carmichael stood silent for an instant looking from one to the other. Then she spoke out very quick as if anxious to tell her story while she could.

'Farewell, master Maxwell! farewell, if indeed you mean to leave us all at such short notice. You shall not go however without knowing my father, my dear father, who has never dared show himself openly in Scotland till to-day. And none of you ever found him out—not even you, with your sharp, suspicious eyes,' here she began to laugh; 'and—and— *Walter*, if I have seemed unkind to you, I am sorry for it now,' here she began to cry, 'and I hope you will forgive me, and love my father as well as I do. My dear, dear father, who has got home safe at last!'

And then she flung herself on the paternal breast and hid her face there, laughing and crying together in a strange, wild mood, very unlike the proud self-reliant Mary Carmichael whose tears Walter had so often wished he had the power to call forth, if only for the pleasure of drying them; but then these natures, like frozen streams melting in the sun, are proof against everything but the warmth of a great happiness.

Sir Patrick Carmichael, for such was the name of Mary's adventurous father, had probably some inkling of how matters stood. Whether she had explained to him that she had a slight regard for this loyal servant of the Queen, or whether, as is more likely, she had confined herself to talking of him on all occasions, and constantly finding fault with him most unjustly rather than not mention his name, is matter for conjecture; but Sir Patrick, grasping Maxwell warmly by the hand, assured him of his own good feelings towards him, and his sincere respect for so brave and devoted an adherent of their Sovereign.

It was this latter quality that had won its way so triumphantly into Sir Patrick's heart. A staunch Catholic himself, Walter Maxwell was probably the only Protestant in Scotland to whom he would have entrusted the happiness of his daughter, but the stout Queen's-man was only bigoted in his loyalty, and he could have refused nothing to the man who saved Mary Stuart from the treachery of her intriguing brother, and the violence of her own subjects.

He had himself been carrying on a secret correspondence with the Guises on the part of his Sovereign for years, a correspondence that involved continual disguises and many hair-breadth 'scapes from the emissaries of those unscrupulous statesmen, who would not have hesitated for an instant to take his life. Such an exploit as the attempt to rob Randolph of his despatches was but an amusing interlude in a career like his, but it was seldom indeed Sir Patrick could enjoy a ride, either for sport or strife, in the society of his own countrymen.

His daily existence was one of imminent peril, only warded off by constant vigilance and acuteness: his only pleasures, and even these were subservient to political purposes, the stolen visits to his daughter, which had so excited Maxwell's jealousy and distrust. He was a bold, nay, a reckless man enough, but he loved that daughter in the corner of his fearless heart better than anything on earth, *except* the cause of his Queen; also, Sir Patrick was a person of delicacy and kind feeling withal, owning that sympathy for a love-affair which those cannot but entertain who have themselves passed, more or less scorched, through the fire.

So he left his daughter and Maxwell together in the gallery, and when they all met at the Queen's table an hour afterwards, he observed that the pair never exchanged a word, but looked as if they had some mutual understanding nevertheless, and were so happy they could neither eat, nor drink, nor converse rationally, nor sit still.

CHAPTER XL.

'I watched her in the morning hour,
　So pure and fresh and fair;
A blossom bursting into flower
　To gladden all the air.

'I marked her shedding sweets around
　Beneath the noon tide ray;
The glory of the garden ground,
　And the pride of the summer's day.

'But long before that daylight's close
　The southern blast awoke,
And crushed and tore the queenly rose
　Beneath its pelting stroke.

'Alas! her petals strew the bower,
　Yet mangled tho' she lie,
The fragrance of the perished flower
　Floats upward to the sky.'

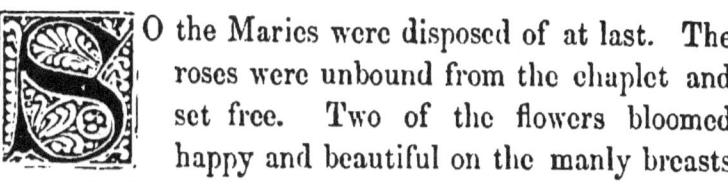O the Maries were disposed of at last. The roses were unbound from the chaplet and set free. Two of the flowers bloomed happy and beautiful on the manly breasts in which they had not spared on occasion to drive their thorns; one clung obstinately to the person of her Queen; and one, perhaps not the least fragrant and fair of the posy, drooped in a cloister, and so withered untimely away.

Mary Hamilton went peacefully to her rest. Mary Seton vowed eternal constancy to her Sovereign, and wished for nothing better than to live and die a maiden in the Queen's service. Mary Beton took her loyal soldier at last, and made him amends, doubtless, for the pain she had inflicted during his probation. Randolph, a little disgusted and a good deal amused, drank a posset to the health of the newly-wedded pair, and even addressed a neatly-turned compliment to the bride, which met with a colder reception than its ingenuity deserved; but then, the diplomatist consoled himself by reflecting that a continuance of his attentions to 'worthy mistress Beton,' as he called her, would be a sad waste of time when she ceased to furnish him with the intelligence he required; and as for marrying her himself, why that of course was out of the question. Ambition is a bride who brooks no rival, and, in good truth, her worshippers cannot have too few ties connecting them with their kind, for they must turn their hands to strange jobs on occasion. Altogether he was well satisfied to see her so comfortably disposed, for Randolph, as has already been stated, was a good-natured man.

Having got over all their differences before marriage, Walter Maxwell and his Mary quarrelled but little after that welcome event. Tried, as their affection had been, in the fire, and proved through so many years of anxiety, sorrow, and estrangement, it would have been unreasonable to doubt it, and madness indeed to hazard such a treasure for the sake of a light word or a moment's discontent. So they went on caring for each other as fondly, though not so uncomfortably, as before.

Neither of them were people to make much demonstration of their feelings, but a calm happiness of repose to which it had long been a stranger, seemed to have settled on the husband's brow, and the love-light still shone soft and lambent in the wife's blue eyes when they turned upon the man she had trusted so long, and so feared to lose at last.

Their time, too, was fully occupied. Plenty to do at home; troubles and strife and stirring news day by day abroad; constant anxiety for the beloved Mistress, whom they were still prepared to serve with zealous loyalty; and no small share of ill-will to sustain from the many disaffected and intriguing, who were never quiet for a day throughout the length and breadth of the land. Nevertheless, of all the Maries, perhaps Walter Maxwell's bride flourished the happiest and the best cared for of the blooming cluster.

But what of the Queen of the Roses, the Mary of Maries, the noblest princess in Europe, the loveliest woman in the world? Alas for the fairest flower in the garden! rain or shine, storm or calm, there was to be no domestic peace, no permanent repose for her. The man who should have tended and cherished her to the death, proved but a selfish profligate, and left her to pine and languish, weary, sorrowing, and alone. The man who would once have shed his heart's-blood freely to shield her from the lightest injury, goaded into madness, ere long snatched wildly at her beauty, soiling her petals with unknightly hand, and dragging the beloved one with him ruthlessly and shamelessly to the dust.

Yet still the stately flower bloomed on, fair and

fragrant under the pure air of heaven, fair and fragrant in the close confinement and the darkened daylight of a prison-house.

But the storm was brewing the while low down in the southern sky; the storm that was about to gather so dark and pitiless, to burst at last in its fury over the Queen of the Roses, and lay that lovely head upon the cold earth, beautiful and majestic even in the pale agony of death.

THE END.

LONDON:
PRINTED BY G. PHIPPS, 13 & 14, TOTHILL STREET, WESTMINSTER.

BY THE SAME AUTHOR.

HOLMBY HOUSE:
A TALE OF OLD NORTHAMPTONSHIRE.
Second Edition.
Two Vols. Post 8vo.
16s.

DIGBY GRAND.
Third Edition.
5s.

GENERAL BOUNCE.
Second and Cheaper Edition.
5s.

KATE COVENTRY:
AN AUTOBIOGRAPHY.
Third Edition.
5s.

THE INTERPRETER:
A TALE OF THE WAR.
Second Edition.
10s. 6d.

GOOD FOR NOTHING;
OR,
ALL DOWN HILL.
Second Edition.
6s.

London: PARKER, SON, & BOURN, West Strand.

www.ingramcontent.com/pod-product-compliance
Lightning Source LLC
Chambersburg PA
CBHW021354230426
43666CB00006B/525